Rediscovering Our Lost Fullness is an important book that will equip people in a practical and biblical way to walk in freedom in an age of sexual confusion. Andrew Comiskey identifies the primary strains of sexual brokenness that plague our society and offers proven solutions toward sexual integration that unites us all in God's mercy. I have known and watched Andy for over 30 years, and he has a long-proven track record of helping thousands of people in profound ways. He is "the real deal!"

—Mike Bickle
Founder of the International House of Prayer of Kansas City

Drawing from 40+ years of marriage after exiting the gay life-style, Andrew is uniquely equipped to speak words of wisdom, affirmation, and truth to those longing for greater wholeness and freedom. This book provides a practical, pastoral approach for tackling the challenges that keep us from living the fullness of the Theology of the Body.

—Dr. Anne Nolte
Executive Director and Co-Founder of the
National Gianna Center for Women's Health and Fertility

In a world of confusion and brokenness, this excellent book clarifies and reminds us of all we were meant to be. Andrew Comiskey so clearly presents the beauty and glory of God's design. He shines the light of God's Word into the darkness, presenting the clear path forward, the way of becoming whole through intimacy with Jesus. What an extraordinary, insight-ful, and timely book this is!

—Julie Hamilton, Ph.D.
Licensed Marriage and Family Therapist, Former President
of the National Association for Research and Therapy of Homosexuality

Andrew Comiskey is a prophet in our own time, speaking God's uncompromising truth with tender mercy to our broken sexuality. Like most good prophets, Comiskey intimately lives his message and so speaks with disarming boldness and humility. Everyone in the Church and our culture needs to read (and live) *Rediscovering Our Lost Fullness*. I loved every page and was challenged to greater integration, personally. I will recommend this book often. It is a wise and tested pathway to sexual wholeness.

—Dr. Bob Schuchts
Founder of the John Paul II Healing Center and author of
Be Restored: Healing our Sexual Wounds
through Jesus' Merciful Love.

Giving voice and a language—born of experience and deep listening to the ache of others and the Heart of the Savior—Andrew's testimony reveals what is possible when we take Jesus at His word. Journeying through his own story out of a homosexual lifestyle and into his true identity as a man made in the image of God, and a good gift for his wife and children, he leaves no stone unturned in addressing the landscape of the sexual and relational brokenness in the culture, in the Church, and in our own hearts. With living hope that mercy radically transforms, Andrew unveils the restorative power of Christ in the Eucharist and in the communion of the Church.

In a culture clamoring and splintered over the body, gender, sex, and marriage, Andrew's testimony invites every soul to a radical transformation through the healing love and mercy born from the side of Christ.

—Sr. Bethany Madonna, SV

In the early 1990s, I picked up Andy's book on sexual wholeness. We were a part of a movement of God that was revealing our need for Jesus and our need for restoration in our lives. Andy's leadership and guidance through The Word and the Living Waters program would touch hundreds or our people's lives and continues to impact us even today. I'm so grateful for Andy's commitment to the Body of Christ and continual pursuit of holiness and restoration back to God's original design for us all. Thank you, Andy, again, for loving Jesus, loving His Church, and loving His people back to wholeness.

—Jimmy Seibert
Founder of Antioch Ministries International
and Antioch Community Churches.

In Gospel terms, an "integrated" life means a "simple" life, a life where all the parts relate to the whole, to Christ, in a harmonious way. In other words, no aspect of life impedes or worse, betrays, the good, noble, and holy purpose that nature and grace intend for each of us. To strive for such a life means first, to stand humbly and courageously in the light of truth, both natural and revealed. Second, it means to love God and His image in others by generosity of heart and self-giving, trusting that when we fall, Christ will raise us up again. Through perseverance and pain, Andrew Comiskey has discovered this path to integrity and simplicity, and his witness will confirm and inspire others to find the peace the world cannot give or take.

— Fr. Paul Check
Executive Director, Shrine of Our Lady of Guadalupe, La Crosse, WI

Exuding the living water of Christ Jesus to Catholic readers about sexual integration, Andrew is candid and eloquent in his treatment of a vital topic. I am certain this book will equip men and women who wish to walk in spiritual clarity on to increasing strength (Ps. 84:7).

—*Anne Paulk*
Founder and Director of the Restored Hope Network

Rediscovering Our Lost Fullness

Andrew Comiskey

Rediscovering Our Lost Fullness

A Guide to Sexual Integration

SOPHIA INSTITUTE PRESS
Manchester, New Hampshire

Cover by LUCAS Art & Design / Jenison, MI

Cover image Apple (61230994) (c) Alex Staroseltsev / shutterstock.com

Sophia Institute Press
Box 5284, Manchester, NH 03108
1-800-888-9344
www.SophiaInstitute.com

Sophia Institute Press is a registered trademark of Sophia Institute.

paperback ISBN 978-1-64413-768-0

ebook ISBN 978-1-64413-769-7

Library of Congress Control Number: 2022943804

First printing

Dedication

To Fr. Paul Check for representing Jesus and Church
truthfully, compassionately, and patiently

Acknowledgments

Morgan Davis, you suffer well with me, a friend like no other. Dino Durando, you ensured a home for us in our diocese, and Fr. Justin Hoye, thanks for opening your heart and parish to Living Waters. Abbey Foard, you believed in this book unlike any other, and Marco Casanova, you worked like no other alongside me to complete it. Greg, Nick, Katie, Sam: you grew up with parents who lived out loud, sometimes to your shame. Thanks. And dear daughter Katie, I am indebted to you for partnering with me in Living Waters and in our Catholic adventure.

Foreword

Rediscovering Our Lost Fullness is a book that can be strongly recommended for any Christian since "all have sinned and fall short of the glory of God" (Rom. 3:23). Andrew Comiskey shares intimate details of his own unique struggles arising from same sex attraction and how, through the love of Jesus and his own wife, he has been victorious in those struggles. The author's dogged determination to be true to what God created him to be — a man — can serve as an inspiration to every Christian facing temptation, any temptation. However, in a day of profound sexual confusion, it is refreshing — and encouraging — to read an author who confidently reminds us, and shows us, that wholeness and joy can be found in being true to God's basic plan for each of us as a man or a woman. The book is aptly described as a *Guide to Sexual Integration* since sin is a disintegrating force in our lives, while God's grace, and our conformity to His will, integrate us and make us whole.

Admittedly, I was somewhat uncomfortable as I started reading the book. My family background is Scottish and German, ethnic groups not known for displays of affection or for sharing personal feelings. There have been intimate moments in our lives about which my wife and I would never speak to others, not because there was anything to feel shameful about, but precisely because they were intimate and personal. How much more would we be disinclined to speak openly of our shameful failings! However, once I became comfortable with the author's style of writing, I found the personal accounts extraordinarily helpful as I reflected on my own struggles with temptation and the temptations of those whom I have counseled. Another fascinating aspect of the book is that it chronicles the journey of a man who began his critically important ministry, Desert Stream, as a Pentecostal and Evangelical (which surely accounts in part for his readiness to share personal matters with his readers) and concluded with his conversion to Catholicism, with its deep philosophical and theological traditions.

The personal, subjective accounts of the author's own life and those to whom he ministers are given a solid intellectual backbone with the incorporation of the insights and order of Pope St. John Paul II's *Theology of the Body* and the Catholic philosopher Josef Pieper's exposition of the four cardinal virtues. Comiskey most effectively applies the profound intellectual clarity of the classical teaching on the virtues to the very personal anecdotes recounted in the book. The subjective and personal are given an intellectual depth and solidity which, had it been lacking, would have been a considerable impoverishment of the insights and lessons Comiskey offers us in his book.

There were so many passages that invited me to reflect on my own past experiences or to connect the author's own profound insights to those I had received from other teachers. I read the sentence, "At chastity's core is the union of sexuality and spirituality, arguably, the two most profound longings of our humanity," and I was very much reminded of the words of Gustav Thibon, "Woman promises man what God alone can give." Woman truly does give man what he seeks, but man's longing (and woman's) is completed ultimately only in the love of, and union with, God. As Comiskey writes, "[God] endows our bodily longing for communion with His beautiful, reordering presence. There lies our hope for wholeness, for becoming an integrated beautiful person whose offering makes others more beautiful too."

In 2014, I was privileged to visit with Pope Emeritus Benedict XVI in his residence in the Vatican Gardens. After the initial pleasantries, he said to me, "The next great challenge the Church will have to face is gender ideology. It will be the ultimate rebellion against God the Creator." Those words came back to me powerfully when I read in *Rediscovering Our Lost Fullness*: "Apparently, the Creator has a will for our sexual humanity. To defy that will is to defy His very essence, His representation on the earth. It also commits what Scripture deems idolatry — thinking and acting as if one knows better than God about His will for humanity. That's why the language Scripture uses to prohibit homosexual practice is strong and framed as rebellion against His natural order."

I have often said that there is only one sex act; it is the marital act. Any other use of our sexual faculties is a disorder and an abuse of those faculties; but it is not sex. I have also often said that there is no such thing as a homosexual. There are only men and women who act in certain ways, with virtue or without virtue. It is instructive that the word "homosexual" does not appear in Scripture. What the Scripture does refer to are sodomites, the active partner, or catamites, the passive partner. The Bible refers to the acts that individuals commit. God created man and woman. Period. There is nothing else. That is why I was so pleased to see Comiskey make this point over and over again in his book: "Integration invited [those of us in healing] to let go of worldly labels and self-definitions. We did not have to hang onto 'gay' or 'bi' or 'trans' or 'adulterer' or 'addict' or 'abused' or 'misogynist' or any identity based on disorder. We learned language that helped us to identify wounds and needs, but we never named ourselves according to those things." We are simply men or women called to glory in and with our bodies.

Rediscovering Our Lost Fullness is an engaging, insightful, provocative, and *very useful* book.

John M. Haas, Ph.D., S.T.L., D.Min.
John Cardinal Krol Professor of Moral Theology
St. Charles Borromeo Seminary
The Archdiocese of Philadelphia

Contents

Acknowledgments. xvii

Foreword xix

1. Mercy, Marriage, and the Real Meal 3

2. Catholic Certainty 17

3. What You Want Is Chastity 27

4. We Need a Community 35

5. Rediscovering Lost Fullness in the Theology of
   the Body 49

6. Marriage and Celibacy 65

7. Prudence and Integration 75

8. Justice and Integration 101

9. Fortitude and Integration 131

10. Temperance and Integration 151

11. Liberating Chastity. 179

About the Author. 195

Rediscovering Our Lost Fullness

ONE

Mercy, Marriage, and the Real Meal

"Husbands, love your wives," says St. Paul.

Simple instructions. But the more I try to love, the less I believe in my capacity to love well. So I go on and read the rest of that passage, and it gives me hope:

> Husbands, love your wives, just as Christ loved the church and gave himself up for her to make her holy, cleansing her by the washing of water with the word, and to present to Himself a radiant Church, without stain or wrinkle or any other blemish, but holy and blameless. (Eph. 5:25-27)

Jesus gave up everything to gain me. He knows that I—like most people—give erratically at best. I'm divided: I long to be whole, but I have impulses that pull me away from my real good.

But Jesus has a plan for us. He envisions something better—a wholeness, an integration, that only He can give us.

I look over at my wife. The blessed face I helped line becomes more beautiful over time and all the more capable of conveying in a glance her sorrow over a slight. More than any other relationship, this one woman gauges the quality of my self-giving. Her face tells truth.

How else can I love others better, especially her, without more of the One who gave all to gain me?

As the religious historian Amy Laura Hall put it, "Love demands of each Christian the disturbing acknowledgement that we do not in the least know how to love faithfully."[1]

Then what can I do? After decades, I'm still only beginning to learn. What I do know is that I can't learn to love without Jesus' help. In the words of St. Bonaventure, there is "no other way except through the burning love of the Crucified."[2]

And even that has been a big step forward.

———

To be fair, I had always loved and looked for Jesus' mercy. I was an obvious sinner—my long history of same-sex attraction and addiction to pornography meant that I had a lot of need for that mercy.

In the late seventies, I was blessed to receive Jesus' embrace through the arms of a young adult congregation called the Vineyard, which had just begun to gather a few miles from UCLA, where I was a student. Pastor Kenn Gulliksen won me over with the well-expressed biblical truth through which mercy ran like a river. He envisaged this Jesus for whom no one is too far gone, who always looks with concern upon our conflicts, and who weeps rather than bristles over our divisions.

---

[1] Amy Laura Hall, *Kierkegaard and the Treachery of Love* (Cambridge: Cambridge University Press, 2002), 24.

[2] St. Bonaventure, *Bonaventure: The Soul's Journey into God, the Tree of Life, the Life of St. Francis*, trans. Ewert H. Cousins (Mahwah, NJ: Paulist Press, 1978), 54.

I remember Pastor Kenn describing a friend of his, an abused woman so wounded that she had begun to identify as a man. She loved Jesus, and Kenn and his wife, Joanie, took her into their small home and just loved her. She made peace with her womanhood when Jesus gave her—through His Church—what she needed: mercy, patience, security, and clarity of identity that only Jesus gives.

From that story, I learned the power of mercy. When God sets the lonely in merciful families, it frees them to *become who they are.*

The transforming power of the Gulliksens's mercy won me over. I'm glad it did. While at UCLA, I was courted by the two most obvious countercultural groups on campus—evangelical Christians and the GSU (Gay Student Union). San Franciscan Harvey Milk had just become the first "out and proud" politician in American history, adding momentum to the LA "gay" scene, which was hip and influential. This posed a big conflict for me. I wanted Jesus—and I also wanted to lose myself in the smart and sexy "gay" scene on campus.

I took a course in "gay" literature and attended similarly themed meetings including, one on "The Bible and Homosexuality." I was frankly unimpressed by the way they majored in "gay" and minored in Jesus. It seemed odd to me that Jesus' call to leave everything to follow Him mattered less to these "gay" Christians than the defining power of sexual attraction. I preached the Cross to them and was kindly rebuffed by most attendees, except one who agreed with me and became a chaste friend.

I was learning how not to be popular.

I realized quickly that unless I found my footing in the Christian community, I would be lost to cyclical partnerships with "gay" peers. I launched into a Christian fraternity where good, conservative men embraced me, and I grew alongside them. All that they asked was that I abide by the biblical boundaries of no sex outside of marriage, regardless of the direction of one's impulses. I agreed.

Perhaps I realized that a solidarity with guys that was based on our common love of Jesus restored something in me. All my life I had listened to an inner voice that told me I was so *different*—so *other*—than "regular guys." Now, surrounded by regular guys, I realized that my pigeonholing them and of me in relation to them, was a distortion of reality, a deception born out of wounding from a few abusive guys.

I came to see, over the years together, that we as men share a common destiny but also differ along a continuum of temperament, aptitudes, and weaknesses. Mine were no better or worse. That was a healing experience.

Back to the Vineyard: I loved this makeshift church. It was a watering hole for many young seekers and highly creative in the way we gathered to tell the truth of our lives and to become agents of mercy for each other in our effort to overcome sin. And I had a lot of sins to overcome! Still prone to porn use and masturbation, and uncertain as to how to navigate strong same-sex impulses, I led some of my brothers in ensuring that all who gathered to grow in holiness did not exclude the harder, more shameful stuff that many were tempted to withhold. How else do we overcome the darkness unless we walk in the light together?

Pastor Kenn also believed in the good of psychological insight in growing as Christians. He encouraged the clinicians among us to share their best understanding of how wounded souls heal, so as to encourage us to bring into light the backstory of our suffering. He wanted nothing to hinder divine mercy in our lives.

I also discovered Leanne Payne at that time. A wise and wonderful literary scholar from Wheaton College who specialized in C. S. Lewis, she had just written a book—*The Broken Image*—on aspects of spiritual and psychological disintegration related to homosexuality. She helped me to piece together frustrating aspects of my early life that contributed to identity distortions. God's mercy worked in a twofold way, helping me to overcome a familiar addiction to sexual sin and to understand my unusual need for same-sex love and attention. Though exaggerated, these needs were emotional and not sexual at all. That realization made all the difference.

The Christian community became a meeting ground for authentic bonds of same-gender friendship. It makes sense: unmet needs from earlier experiences of community combine with rebellious ways of meeting these needs. Trouble. But Heaven comes to earth when a community of mercy gathers to call forth the best in one another. God kissed me with a community of men and a healing church at this formative stage of my life. Jesus' real presence was evident in His members.

Especially one member: a glorious woman named Annette.

———

We both attended UCLA—though we met when she, a manager at the local Christian bookstore, interviewed me for a job. She hired my housemate, not me. Ah well. My zeal for Jesus and His house was a bit much for her, but she relented and nabbed me at the next job opening. We clicked. She needed my zeal to ignite her faith (real but in need of renewal), while I needed her grounded approach to life. She anchored me in our common humanity, while I jumpstarted her reliance upon Jesus. A rich exchange.

That exchange included my opening up to her early on about my same-sex issues. These were deep concerns that I lived with daily and it seemed apt to disclose them in a growing friendship, even before either of us had thought of dating. Annette told me about her older brother whose ongoing homosexual and drug adventures soured her on the subject. The "gay" life had slammed her and her parents. Raised just outside San Francisco, she was no longer enamored with the "free love" sixties but resistant to the overexposed, tripped-out world that had invaded her childhood, and mine.

Annette and I had both been subjected to the sexual "liberties" of the day.

I grew up in a beach town next to Los Angeles. For me, childhood use of porn ignited an early lust that laid a foundation for living immorally. Annette, however, had not only been exposed in childhood to her brother's outbursts and breakdowns, but a visiting relative had raped her when she was four, destabilizing her childhood. As a result, she could not help pairing sexuality with anxiety.

Same sexual revolution, two different impacts: while Annette drew back in defense, I lunged forward, unrestrained. We both needed Jesus and His mercy, though in different ways. It helped Annette when she realized that Jesus wanted a personal relationship with both of us in our darkest areas.

Rather than pleasing God through dutiful acts, religion became for us a community of healing. We learned to draw "water from the wells of salvation" (Isa. 12:3) in our common commitment to the Vineyard Church. We welcomed mercy from Kenn's preaching and counsel; we drank in rain from Heaven as we sang intimate love songs to the Father and Son. Sensitive prayer warriors from the Vineyard exercised gifts of the Holy Spirit that directed our healing path. We grew in wholeness—I discovered good boundaries and emotional objectivity, while Annette found trustworthy relationships that invited her to drop her guard, rebuild trust, and begin to offer her own healing gifts.

Growth came unexpectedly. One night, we set out in Friday night traffic to Santa Monica for an evening of healing and deliverance under the gentle but powerful direction of the Holy Spirit. It would be led by John Wimber, who was already developing a reputation as an important thinker in charismatic circles and would soon be the leader of the Vineyard movement (and a close friend of ours, too).

Annette and I were bickering, and in haste, I entered a parking lot illegally and punctured the car tires. Annette broke down and nearly refused to go into the meeting. Fortunately, her friends spotted her and went with her into the hall, where John Wimber announced he had a word for "Annette." She went forward and, at the altar, God healed her of a lifetime of serious skin disorders. Annette had several psychosomatic conditions due to unresolved stress in her life, and this one He healed through the extraordinary vehicle of John Wimber. Her skin remains clear to this day.

In the meantime, I had to heal my wounded car, which I did with the aid of a former marine (and Vineyard brother) whom I thought I disliked decisively. My opinion of him changed as he helped me do what I could never have done alone. Bless him. Bless God for reconciling me further to the man I was through the mediation of a good and godly man. I picked up a glowing Annette just as the meeting was ending.

I was changing. My housemates became my good friends, and I was becoming a "regular guy" among them. One asked me why I wasn't dating Annette. I did not know why. I was actually beginning to experience a desire for her. Not for all women but for this one. I loved her smell and touch and soft embrace. I missed her when she wasn't around. I wanted her. And I realized all that stood in the way was the belief that I could not relate seriously with a woman because "I was gay." Or had that become an outworn excuse for not wanting to give myself to her or to anyone?

I had grown in fits and starts from child to teen to awkward young adult. My desires were changing. I could not use an old "sexual identity" as a disqualifier. The famous Catholic philosopher

Josef Pieper said, "The sick soul fears more than anything else the demands made on one who is well."[3] I had to face my selfishness. Jesus helped me. The community helped me. Mercy had freed me to forgo habitual masturbation as a stress-reliever and to learn how to open to Annette, express my needs, and listen intently to hers. I wanted to share my life with her! Mercy made the way for us. Annette and I learned that Jesus had to be at the center of our union: we needed ongoing mediation, and He was the guy. We learned to rely upon Him in order to give the other our best. It was a joy—and a challenge—to discover Jesus in this way.

Still, we were weak people, people on a journey, still deeply wounded and each capable of wounding the other. We needed to stand upright in Jesus' firm embrace and love each other. Our love had to come from a growing realization of our dignity as God's children, capable of loving *well enough* but ever in need of mercy.

We dated; we grew together as man and woman. And we started to understand our mission.

———

The beautiful thing about the Vineyard was that each member became a player in God's house. The kingdom of healing and deliverance was not the domain of religious professionals but rather of all Christ-followers. God gave His gifts freely through whom He wanted. We took our places as participants in this "glorious splendor" of His kingdom (Ps. 145:12) and, in the spirit of 1 Corinthians 12, mediated healing gifts.

I recall another visit by John Wimber at our facility in West Los Angeles. He asked Kenn who the leaders of the church were. Good question! Kenn hastily appointed about ten of us who were

---

[3] Josef Pieper, *Faith, Hope, Love* (San Francisco: Ignatius Press, 1997), 119.

present there, including me, and John asked us to come to the front and prophesy over the fifteen persons or so who lined up awaiting my "seasoned" word from the Spirit. I had never prophesied or considered myself a church leader. Come God! Well, I did come to the front, and I found I actually had some clear and specific encouragements for those people. I entered into some kind of glow of the Holy Spirit to build them up in a meaningful way.

In another healing meeting, Annette interceded for persons, one by one. They fell in front of her, resting in the Spirit, and she left a trail of horizontal believes who had been invited by the Spirit to enter into the rest of Him whose yoke is easy and whose burden is light (Matt. 11:28–30).

By this point, Annette and I were engaged. I was in my last semester at UCLA, and Kenn enlisted a seasoned couple to walk with us through our engagement. This couple had faced unafraid the husband's homosexual background; we met together for a year and discovered answers to questions about disclosure, sexual temptation, frustration, arousal, and fulfillment. As for all good marriages, trust and ongoing communication were essential: going forward with eyes and hearts wide open, we were willing to listen and able to speak. And so Annette and I were married; besides following Jesus, that was my best decision ever. United, we served.

Kenn asked Annette and me to help persons facing sexual difficulties in the church, especially those facing same-sex attraction. Our church had grown from one hundred to fifteen hundred in a year, and many who attended were rebels who had come to Los Angeles seeking freedom from traditional restraints and looking for their place in the Hollywood pantheon. Good ground for the

Gospel: Jesus desires mercy, not sacrifice, and He calls broken sinners rather than self-reliant saints (Matt. 9:10-13).

I shared my story one Sunday at church, and the Spirit moved many to come forward with a host of shameful backstories. Included here was a successful designer from West Hollywood—wearied of his old life and expectant of a new one in Jesus—who volunteered his home as a meeting place where any struggler might grow in relation to Jesus.

Annette and I drove up Santa Monica Boulevard from West Los Angeles every Wednesday night for the next two years; we gathered a core team and an amazing group of men and women whom Jesus was drawing to Himself. Many of them were sick and dying and didn't know why—AIDS had not yet been given a name. The Good Shepherd invited them to lie down beside still waters.

That's how we understood our efforts: we focused on Christ Crucified, and sang simple songs of love to Him, and welcomed His Real Presence in our midst. Annette and I liked to think of our gathering as a pool of mercy that deepened with trust and time. I taught, we prayed according to the gifts and leading of the Spirit, and we invited all wounded friends to enter the water. We focused on Jesus as the source that could satisfy our deepest longings. Yet we took seriously the truth that He reveals Himself through one another. Our relational wounds required relational healing.

With every step forward we took two back. I recall dropping off something at a team member's home only to discover him in bed with a friend. When I inquired as to the wisdom of this act, he seemed miffed: "We were only hugging," he said. A participant was so provocative in his dress one evening (he was shirtless and wearing leather pants) that I asked him at the break to consider putting on a shirt. He raced out like a flash, followed by a host of codependent buddies. We lost a few that night.

God took us deeper into His mercy and wisdom. A deaf young man who had been sexually abused in foster care throughout childhood came to the group with the assistance of a female translator who was coming out of a same-sex relationship. He grew fast when people surrounded him with non-erotic love, Jesus style. That's when we realized that our groups needed boundaries that would keep all persons safe from our common sin. So those seriously committed to wholeness started gathering on a Saturday morning for a committed, intensive healing track that we eventually named "Living Waters."

Living Waters became a safe, focused place for those who wanted freedom. Many from that Saturday group built the core team that gave form and order to the later-formed Wednesday group, which was open and evangelistic, full of surprises. One evening, the entire dance team from a long-running stage production showed up. They wanted Jesus, and they wanted to know how He could make a difference in their sexually confusing world.

—

Annette struggled a bit with our colorful cast, as her life had been wounded by sexual immorality. It was easier for her to define herself by what she wasn't—she was neither gay nor promiscuous. Aware during one meeting that she was inwardly critical of the messy lives around her, she heard God's still, small voice: "Do you think my mercy is any less needed by you?" She broke down and wept. She could not stop weeping as she considered how wounded she was and how God had only been kind to her. She needed mercy more than anyone, especially when, in the early days of our marriage, the Spirit invited her to consider a deeper reckoning with her past abuse.

I remember coming home one day and finding Annette in a dark state. She had been crying and seemed almost immobilized, as if something had overtaken her. Usually, these episodes were provoked by something that triggered her: hearing of a child's abuse, the threat of being overpowered by another, or, on occasion, our marital intimacy. Her dark moments were not frequent, but they were consistent. I learned to recognize them and fight through my ambivalence. "This wasn't the bright, smart girl who won me!" I thought.

But my complaining wasn't what she needed. Instead, I experienced the Holy Spirit summoning me to stand and to *love* her—not to react to her, but to reach forward in a confirming and empowering way. My encouragement seemed to dispel some of the bleakness. It drew her out a little bit. I began to realize that she needed the light of my love for her most when she was in the shadows, just as I needed her affirmation most when, in insecure moments, I could be tempted by old lovers. So when the darkness overtook her, I learned I needed to press in, not back up.

Both of us found professional therapists for deeper healing; we were also supported by a group of insightful, faithful friends who gathered to pray for each other weekly. Our own experiences taught us that *anyone* who needed relational healing needed a safe and supportive group. At the same time, we were facing problems in West Hollywood by including only persons with same-sex attraction in our ministry. So we decided to open Living Waters to all persons in need of sexual and relational healing.

We never wanted to lose our edge on ministering hope for persons with same-sex attraction. But same-gender issues were just one aspect of the big issue: traditional offenses between men and women. These less "exotic" sinners from our church and beyond were eager to receive "living waters," too. They saw that our offering was merciful and powerful, an in-depth group designed to keep shameful secrets safe. And because of my graduate studies in psychology and theology, I was able to lend more breadth to the offering.

Annette and I have shared our unique vocation for four decades now; we have offered our still-being-healed lives to equip laypersons to gather responsibly in church-based groups in order to "pray for each other so that [we] may be healed" (James 5:16). Living Waters now flows out on every continent to any person facing sexual and relational sin who wants to grow in Jesus and the wholeness only He can provide—an opportunity to rise and shine for Him and His world.

Annette and I are pleased to have introduced this type of "healing discipleship" to the local church throughout the world; with it, we have helped forge the language of sexual brokenness and wholeness. Most importantly, we have made a case for sexual redemption through Jesus and His Body, doing our part through His mercy to present to Jesus "a radiant church" (Eph. 5:27).

As you can see from our story, our work grew out of the evangelical, charismatic world. Brave were the Catholics who entered our groups and had to translate our traditions into a much older one.

I always admired that bravery. And I was beginning to understand that older tradition. I was beginning to see that there was only one place where the Church itself was not broken, where Christian faith was truly integrated.

TWO

Catholic Certainty

I always loved the quiet depth of my Catholic colleagues in Living Waters. I knew from my liberal arts degree (I majored in English and French) that Catholicism was the foundation of our Western culture. I recognized also, as a matter of fact, that the Catholic Church was the foundation of all other churches and worthy of much respect. Her problems did not bother me. I knew the problems our two-year-old church had. I couldn't fathom the problems of the nearly two-thousand-year-old Bride!

But I had a lot of ties to the Protestant side. What was drawing me across that line to the Catholic Church?

We left the Vineyard movement and Southern California in 2005 after twenty-six wonderful years; we did so with regret but expectancy as we joined Mike Bickle in Kansas City to help build up Living Waters for the flood of young adults joining their 24/7 prayer efforts. We did so gratefully, but we missed regular church life. We joined another local church, a good one, but....

Questions remained for me. What is the Church? What composes her? What holds her together? What defines worship? What defines morality? As a young man, I attributed all church life to movements of the Holy Spirit, who revealed Jesus to persons like me who would not have found Him in a traditional church setting. I am grateful for the pioneers like Kenn and Joanie Gulliksen, John Wimber, and Leanne Payne, who made a way for Annette and me to grow in our salvation and to help others do likewise.

But the here-today-gone-tomorrow nature of many such gatherings troubled me. And I had trouble with the subjective interpretation of truth by my senior leaders. Yes, the Bible is authoritative—but the Bible actually must be interpreted by *people*. I wasn't sure whom I should follow.

Evangelicals value personal freedom and evangelizing the culture. But because of those values, the culture often ends up evangelizing the church. This began to shift the goal posts regarding sexual morality. Many in my evangelical corner became worldly; we assimilated contraception and divorce and began to wonder if "gay marriage" might not be a bad thing for persons with same-sex attraction, who were framed as "born that way," impervious to change.

Could a highly individualistic approach to biblical interpretation hold amid this sexual devolution?

At the same time, I hungered for worship that transcended a string of popular songs. And I grew allergic to one pastor's "leading" shifting the course of our entire church life. I began to find the "free" church disintegrating. Though I loved its freedom to change and rearrange itself, the evangelical church began to lack ballast for me. I wanted a centrifugal force that anchored our worship and our wholeness.

I discovered that my hunger was for the Eucharist. I had a growing love for communion in its diverse Protestant expressions. There I found the connection between Calvary and Jesus' desire to personalize His death and new life in our lives. John 6 always rang true to me, and I approached it as a good biblicist: "My flesh is real food and my blood is real drink" (John 6:55).

Somehow, in the holy meal, God combines the power of His death with the gift of new life. How else can we understand: "Unless you eat the flesh of the Son of Man and drink his blood, you have no life in you" (John 6:53)? Something real is happening here: God takes the work of His Cross and feeds His children through it. The Blood of Christ Crucified shatters the power of darkness. Christ Resurrected empowers us with new life.

I landed on the belief that Communion is the premier expression and experience of the Cross. I was delighted to know that the second meaning of the Greek word for "eat" employed in John 6:53 involves crunching—the use of teeth. How fitting for this meal in which we consume the Crucified One! Deeper still is this mysterious means through which Jesus' Real Presence intermingles with our humanity. He could give no more than He did at Calvary, and He could come no closer than He does in the holy meal. He allows us to consume Him; He hands Himself over, again and again, to become our source. This is divine intimacy, the bond of love that supersedes all others.

I grew to appreciate the Catholic understanding of Communion as I underwent a couple rounds of RCIA, or adult catechesis. I came to love the parish tabernacle that held the Host just beneath the huge Crucifix; Jesus appeared to be descending into bread in order to become our very life. In faith, according to Scripture, I accepted the actual transformation of the elements: I knew now that bread and wine actually become Jesus' Body. I also accepted the prayerful mediation of the priest in that transformation, which integrated the meal with the authority structure of the Church. That made sense to me. Such a high and earthy take on John 6 should involve spiritual authority.

In the meantime, I wasn't ready to take Communion. I had to wait until I was sure of becoming Catholic, just like you wait (or *should* wait) to intermingle bodies with your fiancée until the wedding. It's a huge commitment! You do not commingle with another person only to abandon him or her! If that is evident on the human level, how much more does it apply to the union between a fallen creature and his Creator?

That union applies as well to Jesus' members in the Catholic Church. I loved my evangelical family and friends. I still do. Yet I realized that in becoming Catholic, I was uniting myself with over a billion new family members united by this one meal. Would I be faithful to them, with all the unbelief and scandal and (at times) barely evident devotion to Jesus that marks the historic Church? Would I be true? Could I be?

But there is another side to this relationship. It's not *all* about me. Offering oneself to Jesus and the Church in Communion is surpassed only by His self-gift. He matches our commitment and eclipses it with divine love that burns for us and will not fail us. His flame of love endures for us even when ours flickers for Him. He proved it at Calvary: Jesus' ardent desire to love us through the holy meal cost Him everything. He longs to dwell with us! He wants us!

As I grew in my love of Communion, I realized that Jesus passionately wanted to unite Himself to me.

I love how the Greek word St. Luke uses to describe Jesus' "eager desire" (*epithumias*) to share the Last Supper with His disciples is the same Greek word James uses to describe the desire that lures and entices us to sin, thus bringing death (James 1:14–15). I know something about desire going south. Jesus' passionate longing to become our bread is the antidote.

This is the truth. My life has been defined by the sorting out of conflicting desires, interpreting them correctly, and getting on with the business of loving those I love most, namely my wife and kids. God helps me to offer myself well through the gift of Himself. More than an idea or a historic event, His Body and Blood, shed for me, are re-presented with full effect every time I go to Communion. What a God. What a gift.

Back to my Catholic "engagement." I would show up for the 6:15 a.m. Mass and couldn't understand why the partakers of this most divine encounter were not dancing, falling, swooning, or singing! Okay, okay, this isn't a Pentecostal meeting. But now and again, we need to celebrate God-with-us by using our whole bodies! No one can put that celebration into mere words, though St. Alphonsus Liguori came close: "Ah! My Lord! Who am I that You should so desire to be loved by me? But since such is your desire, I wish to please You. You have died for me; have given me Your flesh for food. I leave all, I bid farewell to all, to attach myself to You, my beloved Savior. My dear Redeemer! Whom shall I love if not You, who are infinite beauty and worthy of infinite love? Yes, my God!"[4]

The famous Catholic writer Jacques Philippe puts it succinctly: "The Eucharist makes clear the degree of intimacy into which God wants to draw us. In the Eucharist, the mad dream of all lovers is realized: to be one in being with the object of our love. God lets Himself be eaten by us: He becomes our substance, and at the same time, He draws us out of ourselves to make us His."[5]

---

[4] St. Alphonsus Liguori, in *Magnificat*, August 2018.

[5] Jacques Philippe, *Fire & Light: Learning to Receive the Gift Of God* (Strongsville: Scepter Publishers, 2016), 111.

As I spent that year in my neighborhood Catholic parish and watched the 6:15 a.m. faithful process before the Cross and tabernacle, and then partake of the essence of the Crucified, I realized that I needed to live in community before the flood of Blood, water and Spirit that is ever-flowing from the Cross (John 19:34; 1 John 5:6–8).

At last came the day when I was ready for love; I was prepared to partake of His Body and Blood and thus unite myself with Jesus and His members. Having taken St. John at his word that through this meal I might actually "live and dwell and abide with Him" (John 6:56) — and then with His Church as well — well, that was not only beyond me but profoundly needed by me.

How else can I live? I cannot do what is good by knowledge or discipline alone, although I value both; I need Him with me and within me — yes, through the Spirit, but more intimately and viscerally, in His very self-gift. As soon as I consumed Him that Easter Vigil in 2011, I experienced a nourishment and composure and source of strength that helped me act a bit more like Himself toward others.

I needed that life. I needed the delivering power of mercy as realized in the holy meal. My spousal union with Jesus through Communion has since possessed a focused aim: to be the best husband and father I can be. That is my calling!

My wife, Annette, could not in good conscience go on with me to become Catholic. That has been hard on both of us, especially her. Yet the truth remains that God has called me to love her above all else and so make evident His love for His Bride, the Church.

That sounds grand, and only rarely do I live up to it. But I know I give better and more consistently when I am rightly aligned with Jesus' self-giving through the merciful gift of Communion.

Early on in my Catholic faith, I heard Jesus say distinctly to me as I buried myself in Edith Stein and St. John of the Cross: "Your first call is to your wife, not mystical experiences. You help each other become saints." I stood upright. Our house church really matters to God. My radical commitment to Jesus and others could and should have one evident impact: giving myself more squarely and purely to wife and kids as a sure sign of Jesus' self-giving to the Church.

For that reason, I love Pope Francis's take on approaching the Eucharist hungrily, weakly, in need of taking hold of what we feel we may not adequately possess. Jesus gives Himself freely, abundantly, in the holy meal. "The Eucharist, although it is the fullness of sacramental life, is not a prize for the perfect but a powerful medicine and nourishment for the weak."[6] Quietly, steadily, this merciful meal renews my love as nothing else does—with Annette as its first fruit. I may walk unsteadily at times, but the strength and impetus to proceed in love is ever new.

Every day, I draw from the diary of St. Faustina, an uneducated Polish nun who, in the 1930s, started a mercy revolution that changed the face of the Church. (Pope St. John Paul II canonized her in 2000 as "the saint of the new millennium.") I know my calling and circumstances are worlds away from hers, but she writes beautifully about the bond of love she discovered in Communion:

> I often feel God's presence in Holy Communion in a special and tangible way. I know God is in my heart. The fact that I feel Him in my heart does not interfere with my duties. Even when I am dealing with very important matters

---

[6] Francis, Apostolic Exhortation *Evangelii Gaudium* (Nov. 24, 2013), no. 47.

which require attention, I do not lose the presence of God in my soul, and I am closely united with Him. With Him I go to work, with Him I go for recreation, with Him I suffer, with Him I rejoice; I live in Him, and He in me. I am never alone, because He is my constant companion. He is present to me at every moment. Our intimacy is very close, through a union of blood and life.[7]

I was going to need St. Faustina very soon.

Jesus' Real Presence in the holy meal became everything to me. It was the antidote to the fallout I received from evangelical family members and colleagues. It was painful to discover that devout friends who welcomed Catholics in principle failed to do so when a close brother became one. Yikes. I had not been expecting that.

Hell broke loose throughout the week that followed my Easter Communion. I was accused of being selfish (true that, but not by virtue of becoming Catholic!). I was even demonized—certain colleagues, who were subject to my leadership, expressed concern over their spiritual well-being. Others just deemed me wrong, misdirected, and foolish. One close family member prophesied that our ministry would perish because evangelicals would no longer finance a "Catholic-run" organization.

Gut-wrenching.

Peace came through daily Eucharist that week and an invitation to attend an afternoon service on Divine Mercy Sunday. The Church invites all members to honor and intercede for mercy, and in particular, the witness of St. Faustina, on the Sunday following Easter. I knew nothing of St. Faustina at this point; I just knew that

---

[7] St. Maria Faustina Kowalska, *Diary of Saint Maria Faustina Kowalska: Divine Mercy in My Soul* (Stockbridge: Marian Press, 1987), 318.

I needed mercy in order to endure the judgment and rejection I faced. I wept through the whole service and eagerly confessed to the priest how my wounded heart could readily harden toward intolerant evangelical friends. In truth, I loved them and fought to stay clear toward them. I received the mercy to forgive them and to allow "the blood and water that gushed forth from the Heart of the Savior" to save me again, to keep me pliable and peaceful amid the fallout.

I picked up St. Faustina's diary that Divine Mercy Sunday and never stopped reading it. It rang true, and loosed a flood of mercy for miserable me. To personalize a quote: "The knowledge of my own misery allowed me to know the immensity of Jesus' mercy."[8] I came to realize quickly that many of my colleagues throughout the world would no longer work with me and that familial bonds would be strained. I also realized that I would have to keep giving an explanation for my decision as well as a doctrinal defense of Catholicism (as if I had the expertise).

Would God's mercy be enough for me to endure this? Tending Living Waters groups around the globe was difficult and controversial enough. Could we be true to our original mission while taking on the Catholic/evangelical divide? Only mercy made a way. My helplessness became the ground for utter dependence upon the Body and Blood.

Jesus spoke these words to St. Faustina, which I heard for me: "Bring your ear close to My Heart, forget everything else, and meditate upon My wondrous mercy. My love will give you the strength and courage you need in these matters."[9]

Mercy is what this book is about. It's about the ordering of our lives according to virtue, which, as defined by Josef Pieper is

[8] Ibid., 56.
[9] Ibid., 229.

"the steadfastness of man's orientation toward the realization of his nature, that is, toward good."[10] But to realize who we truly are and the good for which the Father created us, we need the ultimate virtue; we need mercy.

That is why Pope Francis quotes St. Thomas Aquinas when he says: "In itself, mercy is the greatest of virtues, since all the others revolve around it and, more than this, it makes up for their deficiencies."[11] The theologian Erasmo Leiva-Merikakis (now Fr. Simeon) takes this a step further when he writes: "Without the all-consuming love of Jesus burning in our heart as pure transforming fire, the passions roam the landscape of the soul like ravenous orphans.... Jesus, whose name is 'Savior,' is by definition the source of relief from all oppression, whether self-generated or imposed on us from without.... The opposite of vice in the Christian soul is not virtue but the power of Christ living within us."[12]

What we want is to live a life of virtue—the life God designed us to live. What we want is the happiness that only comes by living according to our nature.

But we can't live that life unless we follow Jesus.

So...

Jesus, lead on.

[10] Josef Pieper, *On Hope*, trans. Sister Mary Francis McCarthy, S.N.D., in *Faith, Hope, Love* (San Francisco: Ignatius Press, 2011), 99.

[11] Francis, *Evangelii Gaudium*, no. 40.

[12] Erasmo Leiva-Merikakis, "Come to Me," *Catholic Education Resource Center*, accessed June 8, 2022, https://www.catholiceducation.org/en/religion-and-philosophy/spiritual-life/the-condition-for-finding-relief.html.

THREE

What You Want Is Chastity

Right on the cover of this book, I promised to talk about *sexual integration*. But what does that even mean?

Integration is the process of becoming whole: how we divided ones become unified in our humanity. What a lot of us have been suffering is *disintegration* – the disunion between what we do and what we're meant to be. It leaves us longing for integration – for wholeness.

When we're talking about sex and relationships, the Catholic word for wholeness is *chastity*.

I see people turn off and shut down when I say that word. Chastity? You mean, like, I have to be a nun or a monk?

But that isn't what the word "chastity" means. Not that it's bad to be a nun, or a monk, or a priest. Those are very good things – but most of us aren't called to those vocations. Chastity is for everyone, and it is a liberation. Once you understand the idea, I think you're going to love chastity. I think you're going to say, "That's exactly what I want!"

Are you saying, "Not likely!" right now?

Well, give me a chance to make my case. Simply put, "chastity" has become for me a marvel of truth, one that unfolds as I walk with Jesus. After over forty years of ministry aimed at redeeming sexual brokenness, I have found chastity to be the most liberating way of conceptualizing what God calls all of His children to realize as men and women.

At chastity's core is the union of sexuality and spirituality, arguably, the two most profound longings of our humanity. We all know the ache: the passion for beautiful presence, enduring, true. C.S. Lewis claims that "we do not want merely to see beauty, though, God knows, even that is bounty enough. We want something else that can hardly be put into words—to be united with the beauty we see, to pass into it, to receive it into ourselves, to bathe in it, to become part of it."[13]

Our yearning for God and our longing for union with others unites with chastity, which the *Catechism* describes as "the successful integration of sexuality within the person and thus the inner unity of man in his bodily and spiritual meaning."[14] Whew. That line will take a lifetime of hits and misses to unpack. Powers of life and love in us drive us. They can deceive us, or they can gently dovetail with this God who loves us enough to awaken a "spring of water welling up to eternal life" (John 4:14) within us, a stream of pure spirituality that somehow becomes the basis for our sorting out the mess we have made of things, sexually speaking.

We can begin with the confession that the beauty we tried to seize enslaved us and further distorted our passions; yet God primed our

[13] C.S. Lewis, *The Weight of Glory* (New York: Harper One, 1980), 42.
[14] *Catechism of the Catholic Church*, 2nd ed. (Washington, DC: United States Catholic Conference, 2000), 2337.

hearts for the greater Love, loosed by our cry for mercy! Now, One greater lives in us who is ever present to help order our sexuality as we devote ourselves to His beauty.

Any Catholic who still thinks that the Father frowns upon sexual desire does not grasp "chastity." God endows our bodily longing for communion with His beautiful, reordering presence. There lies our hope for wholeness, for becoming an integrated, beautiful person whose offering makes others more beautiful too.

Gift begets gift: God's gift in Jesus liberates us so that we have the freedom to offer our humanity to one another. I love how *my* chastity turns into a gift of integrity, of wholeness, to and for *others*. When our spiritual longing for God and His goodness is reconciled to our longing for others, we are whole, united, undivided in our motives, our speech, our behavior.[15] This is simply the fruit of Jesus' self-giving. As His almighty mercy toward us has sought only our good, so we too learn to seek out another's good, denying ourselves when his or her need is greater. Authentic happiness is at stake: "either man governs his passions and finds peace, or he lets himself be dominated by them and becomes unhappy."[16] The unchaste person makes others unhappy in the process as well. Chastity helps guide us as we seek integration: to unite our spirituality and our sexuality. This is a *process*—a long and exacting work, but one made possible by almighty mercy and our efforts empowered by divine strength.[17]

Chastity helped convert me to Catholicism. Here both the fracturing of Protestantism through the homosexual crisis and the help of sound Christians played a crucial role in representing the good news of chastity to me.

---

[15] Ibid, 2338.
[16] *Catechism of the Catholic Church*, 2339.
[17] Ibid., 2342.

Rediscovering Our Lost Fullness

I became a serious Christian during the first round of debates in the historic Protestant denominations over homosexuality. The mid to late seventies sparked debate in the Presbyterian, Episcopalian, Congregational, Methodist, and Lutheran communities over whether homosexuality was disordered in nature and sinful in practice. In a highly politicized move, driven more by "gay" clinicians than hard science, the American Psychological Association removed homosexuality as a psychological disorder from its diagnostic manual in 1973; many Protestants wondered if homosexuality might not be a moral disorder either.

Denominational gatherings nearly choked to death debating this question. Several good books arose from the tension and informed my thinking at this formative time. I needed to know the truth. I was by nature a passionate, subjective person still prone to burning with same-sex lust. It was tempting to line up with "progressives" and assume that I was not *disordered* at all but rather *differently* ordered.

Thank God for Scripture! In light of focused scholarship on biblical references to homosexual practice (Gen. 19; Lev. 18:21; 20:13; Rom. 1:16-32; 1 Cor. 6:9-11; and 1 Tim. 1:8-11), one fact remained: all of these prohibitions or warnings derive their meaning from the truth that same-gender sexuality offends God. Why? It defaces how He chooses to represent Himself in the duality of male and female (Gen. 1:26-27). Apparently, the Creator has a will for our sexual humanity. To defy that will is to defy His very essence, His representation on the earth. It also commits what Scripture deems idolatry—thinking and acting as if one knows better than God about His will for humanity. That's why the language Scripture uses to prohibit homosexual practice is strong and framed as rebellion against His natural order.

Hard stuff.

But knowing the truth invited me into what was most freeing about this biblical exploration: I was a man created for a woman. In spite of feeling otherwise, my essential humanity invited me to accept that I had what it took to be a real gift, not just an awful burden, for the opposite gender.

The Swiss theologian Karl Barth, one of the most influential Reformed thinkers of the twentieth century, wrote brilliantly in his *Church Dogmatics* on God's image in humanity. Unlike many Catholic thinkers who endow the *imago Dei* with abstract philosophical meaning, Barth anchored its meaning in gender duality—true complementarity (not heavy-handed gender-role definitions) that realizes how you are, always and everywhere, a gendered being, and must be true to that reality in how you relate to others—especially the opposite gender. Here, "in this radical sexual duality which is the root of all other fellowship," you discover what you are *not*, the longing for what the other possesses, as well as the gift of your own humanity that can and must be given for the benefit of another.[18]

Sound theology helped me to understand that my goal wasn't just overcoming homosexual lust. It was sexual wholeness—integration and unity within gender differences. My lust simply needed to give way to who God destined me to become in my essential humanity, which, although struck down by sin, was not destroyed. In truth, Jesus was intent on integrating the whole of this still-fractured man. He was summoning the gift He made me to become.

———

Leanne Payne was a huge help to me here. I alluded to her in the first chapter: her contribution to my life and the lives of thousands

---

[18] Karl Barth, *The Doctrine of Creation*, vol. 3 of *Church Dogmatics*, ed. G. W. Bromiley and T. F. Torrance (Edinburgh: Clark, 1961), 167–168.

of others seeking to make sense of same-sex attraction as Christians cannot be underestimated. Leanne saw clearly, as few did, the misinterpretation of homosexuality that was occurring in the late seventies. The church began to mimic the world in ascribing absolute authority to same-sex attraction—making it the basis for a "self" and a community that clamored for ethnic status as if such feelings were inborn, impermeable, and inspired.

A devout Episcopalian, Leanne recognized that this deception would divide and ultimately destroy her denomination. In truth, it has. Most orthodox members have left. Episcopalians led the way in ordaining "gay" clerics and bishops and performing "gay" weddings." Under its rainbow banner, this denomination is slowly dying, as is each historic Protestant denomination that changes the boundary lines of God's will for humanity, made in His image.

Rather than curse the darkness, Leanne ignited the light of truth. I first read *The Broken Image* while at UCLA, and I received more insight on the truth of what my desires meant, and how Jesus wills to redirect those desires, than from any other guide on the subject. Her understanding of disintegration is profound. Who of us will not benefit from her counsel to Matthew? Hounded by homosexual lust, he heard this from Leanne:

"What specifically do you admire in this person [toward whom Matthew was experiencing strong homosexual desires]?"

He replied, "His looks, his intellect, the fact that he is successful."

I then asked him, "What do you do in your fantasies?"

"I want to come together with him. And in my dreams that is what I do."

After the reply, I asked him, "Do you know anything about the habits of cannibals? Do you know why they eat people?"I then told him what a missionary once told me: cannibals eat only those who they admire, and they eat them to get their traits. What was happening to Matthew was very clear: he was looking at the other young man and loving a lost part of himself, a part that he could not recognize and accept.[19]

Leanne linked homosexual desire with the longing for what one feels he lacks in himself, that is, disintegrated attributes of one's personality. The "urge to merge" becomes for the same-sex attracted person a way of "possessing" gender wholeness; as such desire is sourced in a lack of personal integration, its end is hard to achieve. The desired object who seems to embody one's gendered ideal cannot impart that "gift" sexually in a way that actually completes the disintegrated person. In truth, sexualizing those profound needs for gender confirmation may actually further disintegrate the person, as a recent article entitled "The Epidemic of Gay Loneliness" poignantly describes.[20]

For that very reason, Leanne combined her insight on disintegration with Spirit-filled prayer, which God, through sensitive, listening prayers, invites someone like Matthew to recognize, accept, and come together with parts of himself that he was projecting onto another. In other words, Matthew did not need to have sex with a man; he needed to accept the man he was.

Led by the spirit of the heavenly Father, whose confirmation is every soul's most profound need, Leanne taught us to pray. In becoming reconciled to the good gift of our identities as men and

[19] Leanne Payne, *The Broken Image* (Grand Rapids: Hamewith Books, 1996), 46-47.

[20] Michael Hobbs, "The Epidemic of Gay Loneliness," Highline. *Huffington Post*, March 2, 2017, https://highline.huffingtonpost.com/articles/en/gay-loneliness.

women, we were simply less inclined to abdicate our own gender gift by lusting after another's.

Leanne deepened my understanding of the true self, and anchored that self squarely in what the Father, through Jesus, sees in me and says of me. "The healing of man—and his loneliness—has to do with acknowledging himself as a creature, created, and in looking up and away from oneself, from self-worship, to the worship of Elohim, Creator of all that is.... It is in this honest and open speaking relationship that our true self bursts forth, cracking the shell of the old false self; and our old bondages and compulsions fall away with it... Truly to write of the healing of the homosexual is to write of the healing of men everywhere. We are all fallen, and until we find ourselves in Him, we thrust about for identity in the creature, the created."[21]

Taking these insights about gender integration and disintegration, and the Father's confirmation and applying them in the context of Christian fellowship required this truth: yes, I had certain profound needs tied to gender emptiness, but these needs were actually no better or worse than the aspiration for integration, for wholeness, common to my fellow Christians. Perhaps residual same-sex attraction gave me a more acute awareness of my need for integration than your average guy.

I wasn't unique. I wasn't alone.

But I still had to find my place in the Body of Christ.

[21] Payne, *The Broken Image*, 139.

FOUR

We Need a Community

Once I had realized that I wasn't uniquely broken, I had to come to understand how Jesus arranges the members of His Body to make a way for the weak and dishonorable. The Vineyard movement took seriously St. Paul's words about spiritual gifts in 1 Corinthians 12; we highly valued how the Spirit gives these "gracelets" freely to whomever He determines for the sake of building up the Body. "There are different kinds of working, but in all of them and in everyone it is the same God at work.... All these are the work of one and the same Spirit, and he distributes them to each one, just as he determines" (1 Cor. 12:6, 11).

Equally relevant to me was how the Spirit calls each member to come together with the gift of his or her life, and so create a whole. 1 Corinthians 12:12–31 make the strongest case for how personal integration — bodily desire subject to and liberated by our Christian commitment — required an authentic offering of oneself to the one Body.

Aware that either I would worship God at church or I would lose myself to some sexy idol at another "temple," I discovered Jesus in the presence of His members. I was not morally strong or honorable, just open to real love. These verses meant everything to me:

> Those parts of the body that seem to be weaker are indispensable, and the parts we think are less honorable we treat with special honor. And the parts that are unpresentable are treated with special modesty, while our presentable parts need no special treatment. But God has put the body together, giving greater honor to the parts that lacked it, so that there should be no division in the body. (1 Cor. 12:22–25)

Was I one of those weaker parts? Perhaps. At least I know with certainty how much I needed brothers and sisters in my fragmented state. Through them, I committed to wholeness. One tough weekend, I began to prep for a night of partying at a nearby bar. Before I left, a Christian brother dropped by my little apartment. He invited me to dine with him and then go to a local fellowship that evening. Through simply sharing that night with a brother inclined to the Father, I partook of Jesus' provision for me. I slept peacefully and came to understand "division in the body" as what happens to me in the absence of fellowship; when separated from the flock, I am prone to wander and subject to wolves. And I came to see how the enemy of our souls has exquisitely orchestrated another community.

LGBT+ gatherings are based upon "sameness": rallying around our disintegration, especially the ways that we have been misunderstood, misled, bullied, even abused. Often, the Church is villainized as the reason for sexual disintegration and why alternate communities must exist to combat religious "oppression."

Yes, many of us have suffered misunderstandings about our desires and conflicts; some of us have suffered from bad counsel and poor treatment from Christians. But an alternative community based on a shared injury will not set us free. Integration—wholeness—must involve "otherness": those who are different from us and who call us into something more, something greater, through Jesus' Real Presence in their human "gifting." Just as man and woman become the image of God through their difference from each other, so does Jesus summon our best from brokenness as we take our places alongside those whose strength complements weak parts of ourselves, whose clarity lightens dim eyes. They help us to walk further than we could alone or with those sidelined by comparable injury.

Integration must involve the whole body, not a community of one gender or one type of social identification. Wholeness hinges upon our places among *varied* others in our broken, becoming state. That truth informed my integration and my offering of wholeness to others from the beginning.

One of my first pastors eagerly desired to reach persons from the "gay" community; he wondered aloud if it would not be best to gather the gender-confused into a small congregation. Though young and unschooled, I knew intuitively that segregation based on disordered desires defied the biblical mandate for wholeness, and I told him so. A community founded on disintegration cannot heal itself. Yet we agreed that it is wise and good for people to find others who share struggles and understanding for the sake of moving forward. Our first group was primarily for same-sex-attracted men and women who found solidarity with others who shared sexual brokenness and a love for Jesus. We positioned the group as one of a dozen different "home groups" that fed into the sanctuary. We aimed together to integrate into the main and plain of church life, with the help of each other.

How else do we, in weakness, become "indispensable" if we are not known? One of my greatest joys in those early days was to see familiar faces from our West Hollywood group growing in relation to regular churchgoers, many of them families. Others who might never have intentionally befriended persons with same-sex attraction did so and were graced with their many gifts.

Over time, we furthered our commitment to integration by opening the group to persons facing any number of sins against chastity. Sinners wanted in! And we wanted them. Persons with same-sex attraction needed to know that in spite of the depth of their conflict ("intrinsic, objective disorder"[22] — no small cross!), our church was full of folks disordered in different ways.

It healed all of us to gather in our different sins and to discover our common cure: the grace of Jesus released through His large Cross and the beauty of His members. Humbled by our weakness, we got low before Jesus together and discovered there need be no division — neither "gay" nor "straight," "addicted" or "virginal," "abused" or "abuser." We were all disintegrated persons seeking to become chaste in this one Body.

We became more whole as we opened to others whose differences shed light on our paths. One man — a marine outwardly intimidating, and seeking help for being abusive to his wife — provoked to fear three slight men seeking sobriety from "gay" addiction. But as this military guy opened up about his sexual abuse from an aunt and the strange mixture of lust and rage he felt toward women, one of the other men who had been homosexually seduced as an older child helped him connect with the pain and shame of his

---

[22] *Catechism of the Catholic Church*, 2357–2358.

abuse. They prayed powerfully and tenderly for this marine, who began to weep over his suffering and the suffering he had inflicted on his wife. He blessed the group by saying: "You guys think I am the tough dude. I hope you see now that we are all broken; you guys just express it in different ways. Thanks for showing me mercy in my 'normal' sin."

Another man came to the group as he awaited sentencing for child sexual abuse charges. Though he loved Jesus, his moral formation was so weak that he still did not grasp the damage he had done to the most vulnerable. As he confessed to the group that he did not know why he would be sentenced to prison (which occurred a couple weeks later), a young woman from the group, who had identified as a lesbian who was sexually abused as a child, said with tears and gentle firmness: "What you did to that little girl is not unlike what happened to me; it damaged me more than any other injury. Darkness covered me that day, and I face that shadow of abuse daily. Jesus is healing me every day too, but its impact remains. You have cast a big shadow over one who needed your protection. Instead, you took away something she cannot fully recover. God have mercy on you." No one said a word. He started crying; they wept together. We all wept a little. I believe my abuser friend felt God's conviction for the first time.

It was helpful having married and single people together in one group. Same-sex strugglers readily felt disqualified from marriage, a perception that fed self-rejection and pity. It helped them to support people fully committed to their spouses and yet had nevertheless broken vows and trust through their addictions. It was amazing to see same-sex strugglers fortifying spouses and strengthening the fortitude addicts need to live repentance and rebuild trust. That challenged the misperception of same-sex strugglers that marriage is a slick answer to singleness; it takes sobriety, endurance, and much support. It equally challenged the idea that marriage is doomed to failure. Marriages were being repaired in our midst as both parties honestly and persistently practiced repentance and forgiveness.

Rather than feeling disqualified, some same-sex strugglers realized that they were often in better shape to consider opposite-sex relationships than a few of the rather narcissistic addicts who had no trouble with opposite-sex desire. They simply never learned how to love a whole person! Annette and I tried to live transparently, to convey a contoured vision of marital commitment with blessings and struggles (we had four small children in five years). Persons in these early expressions of Living Waters discovered that whether their calling was singleness or marriage, God created them to become trustworthy expressions of His image, male or female.

We were just people seeking Jesus, despite our different divides. He was helping us to identify these barriers to wholeness and to dissolve them so we could offer ourselves better to others. To be sure, it wasn't always easy to assimilate a host of struggles into one group. We had to learn together to persevere and to set boundaries with persons who would not act respectfully to those whose struggles intimidated them. Nevertheless, we felt committed to the biblical mandate of 1 Corinthians 12:12–26—to gather in our differences and to find the one Cross where the weak and shameful might find honor in this one body.

That required a willingness to grow together in empathy and compassion. Each of us had to own our particular struggle. We discovered that each misbegotten identity and desire contained a core longing for security and intimacy that united us all; that truth began to break the grip of accusation and isolation that marked most of our lives. We received mercy from one another and gave it away. In the words of St. Paul: the Father of compassion "comforts us in all our troubles, so that we can comfort those in any trouble with the comfort we ourselves receive from God" (2 Cor. 1:4).

Integration invited us to let go of worldly labels and self-definitions. We did not have to hang onto "gay" or "bi" or "trans" or "adulterer" or "addict" or "abused" or "misogynist" or any identity based on disorder. We learned language that helped us to identify wounds and needs, but we never named ourselves according to those things. Instead, we chose to see each other as new creations—sons or daughters of the Father—members of a royal family through Christ. The fact that we were still inclined to name ourselves according to feelings of illegitimacy necessitated all the more St. Paul's exhortation: "So from now on we regard no one from a worldly point of view" (2 Cor. 5:16). Naming one another according to the truth broke divides in our hearts and hastened our integration as persons.

Gathering as diverse sinners becoming saints freed us from creating a community based on disorder. I could see the temptation toward this at the beginning of Living Waters, when most participants were same-sex strugglers. To be sure, finding persons who shared both our faith and our gender disintegration was a gift: finally, understanding based on shared experience! That can be a blessed relief—but also a burden when we, in our weakness, buy the lie that only persons who sin like us can really love us.

It makes sense. Rejection—real and projected—often defines our lives. We struggle alone with shameful feelings, and then we find solidarity—a community that *gets* our precise conflicts. We can nourish together the lie that "others do not get us," that "normal people will never embrace us." That is a wounded, myopic vision of the Body of Christ. And our healing groups—if not carefully disinfected from this weakness—can even breed contempt for mainline fellowship.

Worse, we can find ourselves falling into old patterns of emotional and physical relations with persons who share our vulnerabilities. I could give you an ugly resume of immoral relationships that resulted from same-sex strugglers who initially started off seeking help. Some were not physical violations but emotional breaches of chastity in which one person inordinately depended upon a specific other who appealed to him or her. That does not occur now. Why? We *integrate*, joining in the harder, deeper task of finding the Cross together from different kinds of backgrounds.

In this task, we also insist on social boundaries that require an "all for one and one for all" mentality in the small group. Each of us forgoes forging one-on-one links and moves forward with a small group of diverse strugglers. That invites one person to focus his or her offering for the group and not just a "special friend"; it also begins to engender the truth that Jesus meets us in deep and mysterious ways through His Body, not simply through that one person who appeals to us. In this, we grow in impartiality and learn to see the witness of Jesus in the "poor" one (James 2:1-4). Rather than nurturing favoritism, we are freed for every member of the group and the unique gift each brings to the whole.

Integration: freedom for the integrity of our own body in the context of the one Body. When he writes to the Corinthians, St. Paul continually juxtaposes one's personal temple with the greater corporate gathering. The one builds upon the other; St. Paul's call upon each member to be pure (1 Cor. 6:12-20) corresponds with his greater goal of a Church that is pure. Together, with each little "temple" doing his or her part, we are built together into something pleasing to God.

In our healing offerings, submitted to Christ, we are seeking to become the Church that presents "her to himself as a radiant church, without stain or wrinkle" (Eph. 5:27). This necessitates integration: not splitting off from each other because of different struggles, but rather gathering in brokenness and discovering a kind of wholeness that only occurs as we enter into the light together.

I can only imagine what a different place our Church and world would be if we discerned fifty years ago what lay ahead when the "gay/straight" divide became evident among persecuted "gays" in the Stonewall riots of 1969 in New York City. A decade later, politicized "gay" segregationists challenged each mainline Protestant denomination, insisting on "gay" rights on par with those "straights." Roman Catholics took a different tack in the aftermath of Vatican II in the late sixties. Unable to change Church doctrine, many priests simply adopted "gay" liberties: shadowy, foul behavior that resulted in the violation of scores of male teens, the people group most represented in the comprehensive John Jay report that charted clerical sexual abuse from the later part of the twentieth century.[23]

You might say that homosexuality split the Church, beginning with the splintering of the Protestant denominations and slowly infecting the Roman Catholic Church, if nearly daily revelations of uncovered clerical abuse count. Disintegration—the tearing apart of lives and the life of the Church—has always been the enemy's goal for us, the Body of Christ.

Perhaps we have not fully grasped how effectively the devil has used homosexuality to disintegrate lives and divide us. He continues to do so with a vengeance. The Church is still lured by this alien anthropology; a 2018 Synod of Bishops on Young People, Faith, and Vocational Discernment became a battleground

---

[23] The John Jay College of Criminal Justice, *The Nature and Scope of Sexual Abuse of Minors by Catholic Priests and Deacons in the United States 1950–2002* (February 2004), distributed by the United States Conference of Catholic Bishops.

between LGBT+ special interests seeking confirmation and the orthodox.[24] Daily, baptized youth come home from Catholic universities and "come out" to faithful parents as members of a queer or transgender "ethnos."

———

How do we best combat this disintegration and the division that naturally results from this faux anthropology? We begin as members of Christ who own our sins and gather courageously to overcome them. We neither minimize nor dramatize them, but yield our sins to the One who "gave Himself up for her [the Church] to make her holy, cleansing her by the washing with water by the word" (Eph. 5:25–26). Persons dealing with sins related to gender identity would have no trouble "coming to the water" if secrets and lies tied to more traditional sins were repented of regularly and thoroughly.

Those who have been abused would come forth readily if we owned how deep this wound is and admitted the shameful silence that has accompanied it. The same applies to the congregant on his second or third marriage, the porn-plagued youth, the boozy misogynist or loose woman, the cohabiting couple, and other men and women who have simply messed each other up; we must acknowledge the main and plain of our wounds, discover ways to own our corporate brokenness, and gather to heal.

For that reason, I tend to discourage persons with same-sex attraction from seeking each other out as the primary vehicle for restoration. Even in recovery, I believe it works best to integrate and discover wholeness together with our different sins and gifts. We must dig deeper and find our common quest for love, laboring

---

[24] Charles Chaput, "Synod 2018: Some Concluding Thoughts," *First Things*, October 29, 2018, https://www.firstthings.com/web-exclusives/2018/10/synod-2018-some-concluding-thoughts.

together to rend the veil of shame and resist false solutions for real needs. I have walked years in such groups: integration, not segregation, represents best God's heart for healing the unchaste in whatever ways we find ourselves divided.

Integration does something else: it sets in motion God's plan. He wants to take this one problem of same-sex attraction that in its misinterpretation has morphed into LGBT+ madness and turn it around. Through almighty mercy, He takes what the enemy has used to divide and, through transforming love, invites all who seek to heal.

That's what I see in our groups. We who struggle with gender-identity issues own our stuff: the early abuses, the breakdown with loved ones, early patterns of addiction, rebellion against tradition, and the lure of the exotic. We must face the depth of this struggle. For many of us, this is not passing fancy—it is deep and rooted in real distortions of thought and emotion. And it is immoral, a profound disorder that blocks us from engendering real life in our love of God and others.

Disintegration costs us dearly. But now, turning back to Jesus, scores of men and women have forsaken "selves" tied to LGBT+ unreality. And we are discovering our places as healers in the Church. We listen to the true Word that defines us as sons and daughters of the Father, growing as good gifts to each other in our gendered selves. We are learning to hurt at the foot of the Cross, to heal through extending forgiveness to our captors, and to be reconciled to loved ones. As Jesus slowly but surely unites us in our pretty-good humanity, we call others to join us in becoming whole. Disintegration cannot prevail when we humble ourselves before each other and learn how to pray effectively for each other.

In this way, we keep our wounds and weaknesses free from dirt. And we discover something else: there is no such thing as

"LGBT+ persons," just people like us who lost the track of truth, who settled early on cultural lies, who mistook early dents in our humanity as our destiny, and who then confused sex with needs related to same-gender identification and intimacy. Deep stuff. But Jesus' mercy is deeper still, breaking confusion and deception and turning our troubled lives into a fountain of hope for others. *All* others—not just fellow gender-benders but all who in the believing community have stopped becoming the good gifts they are.

How else can I understand Daniel? As a boy, he coped with chaos by sexing it up with guys while he fantasized himself to be a glamorous girl. Competing in drag pageants, he saw clearly the culture of death surrounding him (drug addiction, suicide, and murder) and returned to the love of a Christian church family. Many years later, with years of integration under his belt, he stands as a beacon of healing for persons in his local church.

Or Amanda? She threw herself into a series of illicit same-gender relationships—and then, coming up empty, returned to the Jesus of her youth—but as a wounded adult who needed healing from a distorted vision of women and an abusive view toward men. Today, still healing but on a solid track of truth, she leads a dynamic group for healing any disintegrated person in her church who wants "to come to the water."

Two people surrendered to Jesus, hundreds more enlivened by the almighty mercy that became their freedom—living waters still rising from their depths and now from their communities of faith. These two (and scores of friends like them) fulfill Leanne Payne's words: "To speak of the healing of the homosexual is to speak of the healing of all persons everywhere."[25]

[25] Payne, *The Broken Image*, 139.

The enemy's efforts to divide the Church through homosexuality will be overcome by formerly divided people who now live the truth in love. Taking our places in the Church, we shall secure many who are being tossed about by LGBT+ unrealities. "Then we will no longer be infants, tossed back and forth by the waves, and blown here and there by every wind of teaching and by the cunning and craftiness of people in their deceitful scheming" (Eph. 4:14). Demonic disintegration is no match for those being redeemed by divine mercy. Jesus works a greater good than the evil intended by the enemy. He invites each of us onto the path of integration. He frees us from disintegration as we walk together—one people, one Baptism, one Father of all mercy, one step at a time.

So I had learned that my own sins were disintegrating—that they pulled apart what was meant to be together. I knew that I wanted the wholeness that God had planned for me.

But what would that wholeness look like? I had so many questions.

And just as I was asking them, John Paul II came along with exactly the answers I was looking for.

FIVE

Rediscovering Lost Fullness in the Theology of the Body

While in seminary during the eighties, I found the words to explain what it means to be human, to be made in God's image.

This was a gift to me from Dr. Ray Anderson, whose doctoral studies in Europe had centered on the great Swiss theologian Karl Barth. Both men opened my eyes to a holy understanding of gender. I learned a new term—*theological anthropology*—that became a gateway for discovering how God deepens and sanctifies humanity through a commitment to working out our lives together, particularly with the opposite gender.

This confirmed and deepened all along what I had experienced in shedding my "gay" self and shouldering the gift and responsibility of marriage. As I sought spiritual strength in community to love this one woman, I became more of a man. And she became more of a woman. We were two distinct human beings, but love made us a pair—and that made each of us more fully human. God, who made us for each other, compelled us to give and receive from one another more than we thought possible. Yes, we were the ones who loved, with the whole of our fragile selves. But something divine kicked in that consumed the sacrifice and made it burn. This was God's call for Annette and me: to tend to the flame fueling our domestic church and to welcome others into its heat and light.

It was hard. My moderately conservative seminary was also in the vanguard of biblical feminism. That was a good thing in light of chronic misogyny, but it was dangerous in its tendency to obliterate gender distinctions, to write off any talk of essential masculinity or femininity as oppressive to women. Such championing of woman paradoxically erased both her meaning and that of her male counterpart. This resulted in a new openness to blessing "gay" unions and ordaining "gay" clergy. Why not? If gender distinctions are mere socially constructed injustices, why not cast them off and open ourselves to other sexual possibilities?

Jesus anchored me in marriage—and in Karl Barth's anthropology, which provoked me to probe the combustion, fruitfulness, and fullness of life I was discovering with Annette.

I needed that anchor. A visiting scholar did a series of lectures on how the image of God in humanity should be understood only in terms of love, not gender. I knew implicitly that his intention was to be inclusive of all couplings, a hunch that proved true as he urged his Protestant denomination to ordain "gay" clergy and marry "gay" couples.

Further, a married and much-loved professor from the seminary had just left his family for a man and claimed that he was finally being "true" to himself. He divorced, and he influenced many from the seminary who loved him and felt sorry for him—while overlooking his wife and kids, who were most afflicted by his history of homosexual addiction.

The "coming out" of several Christian leaders afterwards further eroded the seminary's faith in Jesus to help His human creation live in accord with God's design; many wondered if perhaps there were several sexualities God might bless. One renowned professor greeted me in the hallway with a question: "When are you going back into homosexuality?" — as if any attempt to walk in integrity as a faithful married man was futile.

The leaning tower of Protestantism — how long until it fell, and the torch of what it means to be human was extinguished?

I read *Humanae Vitae* (Of Human Life) by Pope St. Paul VI, the 1968 encyclical that refused to "go with the flow" of the sexual revolution. I was intrigued by the force with which its author fought for marital love and refused to separate intercourse from child-bearing (the *unitive* and *procreative* aspects of intercourse). That was strangely new to me. My studies had emphasized the unitive nature of man and woman — how their differences complemented each other and intensified intimacy — but they were silent about cultivating openness to creating new life.

It did seem odd to me, and rather weak, to base an anthropology on the duality and communion of man and woman while de-emphasizing its fruit — children. Further, in my evangelical circles, we simply assumed contraception was the norm. Premarital counseling invited discussion about how the couple might plan wisely for family life, employing whatever method desired to prevent pregnancy until the chosen season for children.

I began to see the limits of my moral thinking here. Given the debate over the validity of "gay" unions at seminary, I wondered if separating the unitive dimension of marriage from the procreative weakened the theological defense of God's image as male and female. If blessed union did not have an end other than "love" as one understands it—in other words, if kids were optional and in their place was just my idea of pleasure and partnership—why wouldn't Jim and John be on par with Jim and Jane?

Early on, Annette and I employed contraception due to the demands of full-time ministry and seminary. We succeeded only in conceiving new life. Condoms and pills were no match for fierce sperm and eager eggs. We ended up having four kids in five years. Whew! We never had enough money or time. But grace prevailed, and we discovered that our union was as much (or more) about these new lives we made and reared as about our aesthetic or psychological appreciation of each other. In those days, our sweet, noisy clan prompted most people to assume we were Catholic. Perhaps we were on the way. You could say family life was converting us.

I gave more thought to Catholicism as I considered the theological nature of humanity in general and of marriage in particular. The thoughtful solidity of works like *Humanae Vitae* intrigued me. Divorce was a common solution in our youthful California churches; I struggled to find any New Testament rationale for dissolving marriage, as well as for the increasing tendency of persons with same-sex attraction to "gay-identify" and seek "gay" unions. The Bible was badly invoked to justify immorality. I loved Scripture—much of my seminary education was about ancient languages and good exegesis. But the Bible must be interpreted, and I was surrounded increasingly by worldly guides.

But Pope St. Paul VI refused to separate the unitive and procreative aspects of marital love. He invoked the Church's courage to uphold "the whole moral law" because "of such laws the Church was not the author—she is only their depository and interpreter."[26]

---

[26] Paul VI, Encyclical Letter *Humanae Vitae* (July 25, 1968), no. 18.

It was my first glimpse of the Church as guide and guardian of theological and anthropological questions about humanity. Until then, I had only known various theologians with various viewpoints, none binding. I liked this new idea of the Church as a cohesive moral source.

After seminary, I was blessed to meet a young theologian, Christopher West. He was then the head of Marriage and Family Life in the Archdiocese of Denver; we were doing one of our "Pursuing Sexual Wholeness" conferences in his city. He attended the conference and handed me a large, theologically dense volume of Pope St. John Paul II's *Theology of the Body: Human Love in the Divine Plan.* West is himself a masterful interpreter of John Paul II, but West's impact as an educator came later when I attended a series of weeklong lectures at his institute. I remain indebted to him for first handing me a copy of *Theology of the Body* and a related document, *Mulieris Dignitatem* (On the Dignity and Vocation of Women.)[27] Both these works had a converting effect on me.

———

Over the next two years, on planes and trains and in waiting rooms, I consumed *Theology of the Body.* I wrote my own small companion guide in the notes I took, which I have read and reread over the years. To me, the Theology of the Body sang God's love song for humanity, music that invites us to the challenging and splendid dance of offering our sexual gift to the other. Rather than ponderous, I found it lyrical and worthy of slow meditation.

Not only did the Theology of the Body draw me closer to Catholicism, but it also anchored me in a deeply spiritual and incisive understanding of man for woman and woman for man—the ordination

[27] John Paul II, Apostolic Letter *Mulieris Dignitatem* (August 15, 1988).

of our gendered selves and the diminishment of the threat of lust. Most importantly, St. John Paul II's excellent work highlighted the redeeming power of sacramental marriage and Jesus Himself, who frees humanity from the dominion of disorder, so that we can find something like genuine happiness in human relating.

Practically, I developed a more attentive, tender, and active posture toward Annette. Academically, the Theology of the Body took what I had learned previously and crowned it with an unparalleled authority and compassion. I'll try to describe its impact more thoroughly.

St. John Paul II undertook the formation of the Theology of the Body as a series of weekly lectures in Rome over a five-year period, from September 1979 to November 1984. I did not realize until the end of the book that his express purpose in creating the Theology of the Body was to provide an extensive commentary on *Humane Vitae*[28] and, more particularly, to formulate a biblical theology that would support, nuance, and strengthen Pope St. Paul VI's (comparatively brief) effort to fuse the unitive and procreative aspects of marriage.

During the Theology of the Body's long formation, Pope St. John Paul II had his hand on the frantic pulse of a culture more sex-saturated than ever yet less loving to its young. Perhaps he was prophesying a living, breathing witness of chaste sexuality for generations to come, in the hopes of impacting who man will be for woman, and woman for man. In me, a married man still vulnerable to lust, yoked to a fine wife, raising a family of four, and ministering full time to persons bearing truckloads of sexual baggage, Pope St. John Paul II had a rapt audience.

---

[28] John Paul II, *Man and Woman He Created Them: A Theology of the Body* (Boston: Pauline Books and Media, 2006), 133:4

St. John Paul II's vision and version of sexual chastity is undergirded by radiant spiritual chastity. A river of living spirituality runs through this work that can only be attributed to his dynamic, lived experience of faith in Jesus and His friends. I came to understand that John Paul II was steeped early on in Carmelite spirituality, especially in the works of St. John of the Cross. Perhaps the latter reinforced in St. John Paul II the truth of full espousal to God—holding nothing back in intimate self-giving to this God who is unashamed to call Himself our Bridegroom.

This spousal dimension of personhood runs throughout the Theology of the Body, and is spelled out explicitly in *Mulieris Dignitatem*. There John Paul II links union with God as the basis for our dignity as human "gifts"—gifts both to God and to each other. Mary, Mother of God, exemplifies this union in her complete yes to God and thus becomes for John Paul II the "representative and archetype of all humanity, both male and female";[29] he does not shy away from imploring all of us to behold in her the feminine principle of responding to God—offering ourselves to Him—as the essential feature of our spirituality and our human dignity.

As the "most complete expression of this dignity and [maternal] vocation,"[30] Mary exemplifies how the Church becomes a mother like herself; together, members of Christ bring forth spiritual children through the brooding power of the brooding Holy Spirit. Mary, perfectly pledged to her Son, exemplifies this motherhood, as must we if we are to be fruitful.[31] So Mary figures big as a model and guide for Christians in understanding who we are as the Church, espoused to God and generative only in response to our Bridegroom.

---

[29] John Paul II, *Mulieris Dignitatem*, no. 4.
[30] Ibid., no. 5.
[31] Ibid., no. 22.

That blew me away. I had always loved Mary, but St. John Paul II highlighted her gift in a way that illuminated *my* gift. Mary is the model and guide for all who seek to be gifts to each other. Men seeking wholeness need Mary's heart. And I, a seeking Christian, was brought closer to a distinctly Catholic understanding of "church" that has at its core a profoundly spiritual anthropology for her members that begins with the Marian heart.

So St. John Paul II clarified to me the theme of "gift"—God's fundamental gift-giving in Christ, through Mary, to us. Spiritual chastity involves becoming rooted and grounded in that gift of love.

> I pray that out of his glorious riches he may strengthen you with power through his Spirit in your inner being, so that Christ may dwell in your hearts through faith. And I pray that you, being rooted and established in love, may have power, together with all the Lord's holy people, to grasp how wide and long and high and deep is the love of Christ, and to know this love that surpasses knowledge—that you may be filled to the measure of all the fullness of God. (Eph. 3:16-19)

Throughout the Theology of the Body, St. John Paul II takes deeply spiritual realities and insists that these are meant to be touched, tasted, and lived. The lived experience of authentic faith matters to him; our freedom to offer ourselves to others hinges upon living communion with Jesus and His friends.

St. John Paul II writes: "Man must, so to speak, enter into Him with all his own self, he must appropriate and assimilate the whole of the reality of the Incarnation and redemption in order to find himself."[32] The deeply personal matter of receiving the gift of God

---

[32] John Paul II, *Man and Woman He Created Them*, 86.

and becoming a gift to others is founded on faith, a faith "that must penetrate and transform human experience. It must be received and enriched in the lived experience of personal subjectivity."[33]

I came to understand St. John Paul II's ethical basis for hearty engagement with the opposite gender as founded on this philosophical strain of *personalism*.

What is personalism?

Humanae Vitae and the Theology of the Body are founded upon a high and profound understanding of what it means to be human—the dignity God built into His human creation, and the dignity with which we are to uphold others. Personalism, then, has to do with what corresponds to our essential dignity, what we can be and do and become in relation to others. I choose the word *"becoming"* because the Theology of the Body insists that *Humanae Vitae* is a *pastoral* encyclical, designed to help married couples live the unitive and procreative aspects of marriage. In that way, the Theology of the Body serves *Humanae Vitae* by emphasizing the dignity of man for woman and woman for man and then encouraging the couple to realize that dignity.

While highlighting human dignity on the one hand, "personalism on the other hand helps people to realize that dignity as an authentic interior process of development."[34]

Christopher West highlights John Paul II's distinction between *ethos* and *ethics*. While taking ethics seriously—the objective law, like the indissoluble nature of the unitive and procreative meaning of marriage—John Paul II insists on the proper "ethos" of

[33] Ibid, 87.
[34] Ibid, 133:3.

redemption—"which refers to a person's subjective world of values,"[35] "the inner form of human morality."[36] Redemption in the Theology of the Body thus involves a process whereby "the subjective desires of the heart come in harmony with the objective norm."[37] In other words, you come to *want* what is objectively *right*.

I love this "personalism!" How else can we engage authentically with God and others on where we are in light of what Jesus wants us to be? The Theology of the Body invites us to consider that God cares about the inner process—the contradictions, conflicts, steps forward, and steps back. For anyone battling life-defining strongholds of disorder, "knowing the truth" is insufficient. The *ethic* (objective truth) can hang like a sword over the earnest infidel until he or she discovers this *ethos* of redemption. Through that ethos, Jesus invites us to sort out our inner strife in the light of Jesus so we can realize the truth. We are becoming dignified, and we are growing in our capacity to dignify others.

I rejoice in this. But I know that the high calling requires many steps and much mercy for missteps.

Personalism demands that you personalize *your* route to growing as a gift designed to dignify *others*. I take it seriously when St. Paul exhorts us to emulate Jesus' generous self-giving toward the Church: "Husbands, love your wives, just as Christ loved the church and gave himself up for her to make her holy, cleansing her by the washing with water through the word, and to present her to himself as a radiant church, without stain or wrinkle or any other blemish, but holy and blameless" (Eph. 5:25–27). My

---

[35] Christopher West, *Theology of the Body Explained: A Commentary on John Paul II's "Gospel of the Body"* (Boston: Pauline Books and Media, 2003), 36.

[36] John Paul II, *Man and Woman He Created Them*, 24:3.

[37] West, *Theology of the Body Explained*, 36.

long-term goal is to make us radiant in love according to Jesus' example. But every time I think about that goal of giving freely to Annette, I must confess how halting my efforts are—one step back, two steps forward.

My "subtext" of same-sex attraction—the way that I, in weaker moments, may be inclined to sexualize masculine strength—requires me to be constantly aware of my interior life. Alert to obstacles on the path, I can offer them to Jesus and friends quickly while securing the necessary encouragement to proceed robustly in love.

It works! Personalism helps launch the good intentions of weak persons like me into action.

And act we must. St. John Paul II makes clear in the Theology of the Body that Jesus "assigns the dignity of every woman as a task to every man," and vice-versa, in how we love this other with the whole of our flawed humanity.[38] No small call!

———

The Theology of the Body begins by laying out three "words" of Jesus that anchor this call to dignifying the other through one's self-gift in the Gospels.

In the first, from Matthew 19, Jesus redirects the Pharisees' wrangling over divorce to "the beginning":

> Some Pharisees came to him to test him. They asked, "Is it lawful for a man to divorce his wife for any and every reason?"
>
> "Haven't you read," he replied, "that at the beginning the Creator 'made them male and female,' and said, 'For this reason a man will leave his father and mother and be

---

[38] John Paul II, *Man and Woman He Created Them*, 100:6–7.

united to his wife, and the two will become one flesh'? So
they are no longer two, but one flesh. Therefore what God
has joined together, let no one separate."

"Why then," they asked, "did Moses command that a
man give his wife a certificate of divorce and send her away?"

Jesus replied, "Moses permitted you to divorce your
wives because your hearts were hard. But it was not this
way from the beginning. I tell you that anyone who divorces
his wife, except for sexual immorality, and marries another
woman commits adultery." (Matt. 19:3-9)

When Jesus says "from the beginning," he's referring to Genesis
1-2, in which humanity is set apart from the whole of creation as
bearers of God's image—a calling that has everything to do with
launching out into communion with this gendered other. "One
becomes the image of God at the moment of communion."[39] Here,
St. John Paul II weaves together themes important to the Theology
of the Body—the inseparable nature of body and spirit, and how
Jesus (God-in-flesh) frees us to recognize "in the beginning" the
beauty of the body as an instrument of love and dignity, rather
than of lustful manipulation.

Much is made in the Theology of the Body about "the spousal
nature" of the body—its capacity and call to express love for this
other.[40] St. John Paul II invites us to view this bodily "gift-giving"
through the lens of Jesus, and it is very good. Here is mutuality
in difference, a seamless fusion of body and spirit, and an offering
of self that is aimed at the happiness of the other person: in other
words, sexual love, which renders the union indissoluble, open to

[39] Ibid., 9:3.
[40] Ibid., 15:1.

life, and dignifying of all persons influenced by this union. The Theology of the Body elevates and deepens how we understand ourselves as "bodies" designed to be gendered gifts for the other. Early on as an evangelical, I had learned from Barth that gender duality was an essential property of bearing God's image. That challenged me to pursue further integration as a man and to offer myself responsibly to a woman. Yet the Theology of the Body offers a richer vision than Barth in directing us to the garden via Jesus' words in Matthew 19. Already, we sense that redemption is at work in us as we consider what it means to fulfill the divine call with our bodies. Divine love does more than invite us to consider gendered gift-giving: it helps us to do so with love governed by *self-control*, an even-handed approach aimed at seeking the other's good.

Self-control implies that the river of our sexuality is prone to corruption—to flooding over its banks. We all live east of Eden now. We are still the very good creation envisioned by God in Genesis 1-2, but we are hammered by the Fall in Genesis 3 and the shattering of our image. We see through a cracked lens as we behold our fellow humanity, and we're aware that our gift-giving can either fracture or free others.

Pope St. John Paul II helps us here by directing us to the Sermon on the Mount for his second round of Christ's words, emphasizing the "adultery of heart" common to humanity in Matthew 5:27-28: "You have heard that it was said, 'You shall not commit adultery.' But I tell you that anyone who looks at a woman lustfully has already committed adultery with her in his heart."

Here, St. John Paul II helped me considerably by widening and deepening my understanding of such "adultery." Referring to it as lust, or concupiscence, John Paul II casts a broad net that catches a range of wild desires, all sourced in Original Sin. While Genesis 1-2 offered integration of body and love, the Fall collapses both the freedom to accept the body and to give oneself generously and sincerely.[41] Sin disintegrates: instead of releasing the other to freedom, one grasps the other in selfishness. The gift of self becomes reduced in how one regards self and others.[42] Whereas love is expansive, St. John Paul II describes lust as reductive, a vice that conforms another to one's own stingy image rather than contributing to the dignity of being made in His.

This blessed me in three ways.

First, for St. John Paul II, lust is an equal-opportunity offender. Adultery of the heart flares up in all of us in myriad ways. That helped me as a same-sex-attracted person who often feels as if his "flare-ups" are more disordered than those of traditional idolaters. I do not feel a trace of that in John Paul II's writings. I am just a normal expression of God's image, with a unique chink in my armor born from the disorder common to all.

Secondly, John Paul II makes clear that "the man of lust," every man and woman, "is also capable of discerning truth from false-hood in the language of the body."[43] Something deeper remains in us, which has its source in Paradise, in divine order. Aware of lustful detours, we can know the truth of what we are *for* and live that out. Lust does not have the last word—love does.

This brings me to the third point—redemption. Jesus' love surrounds and redeems the adultery written on our fallen hearts. The Sermon on the Mount probes the depths of familiar sin while inviting us to the One who fulfills His law of love in our very members. To be sure, redeeming these bodies occurs over time and

---

[41] John Paul II, *Man and Woman He Created Them*, 27:4.

[42] Ibid., 28:1.

[43] Ibid., 107:5.

with effort as we engage with God and others "in the exclusively inner movements of the human heart."[44] Still, we do so as sons and daughters of the One, not as slaves to lust.

Our participation with Christ in "getting back to the garden" is all about redemption, moving forward into our new way of life of self-control and purity. Jesus grants us that new life as children of the Father, through the Son, in the Holy Spirit. Both self-control and pity quicken integration as we accept the gift we are and learn to offer that gift well.

———

Now we come to the third "word" of Christ that informs St. John Paul II's redemption of the body. This one involves resurrection: here Jesus' words invite us to discover the limits of marriage. "At the resurrection people will neither marry nor be given in marriage" (Matt. 22:30).

Something is going on here. The glory of marriage on earth lies in its pointing beyond itself to a heavenly consummation — the wedding feast of the Lamb — when all the faithful shall be permeated with divine love.

I love this little saying. It frees us not to make marriage an idol, but rather a window or an icon that directs each of us to the greater good and goal of union with our God. Just as my parents revealed something heavenly to their children, I trust that my wife and I, in our fidelity, reveal something of His spousal love for us all. Everyone — single or married — longs for face-to-face communion with the living Bridegroom.[45] This future hope will involve our male and female bodies that, glorified, will fully realize the "spousal

[44] Ibid., 86:6.
[45] Ibid., 67:5.

meaning of the body" as we enter into perfect communion with our God.[46] Imperfect though it is, marriage on earth possesses heavenly meaning!

And according to St. John Paul II, so does inspired celibacy. Celibacy and marriage go together in ways I had never thought of before.

[46] Ibid., 69:4.

SIX

Marriage and Celibacy

The Theology of the Body links future resurrection with the call today to celibacy for the Kingdom's sake. In other words, some persons who choose spiritual intimacy and service over marriage reveal something profound about the future—they are a glimpse on earth of the glorification of the body to come.[47]

I had never heard this put more clearly and hopefully; it ascribes beauty and purpose to persons whose singleness demonstrates "a special participation in the mystery of the body's redemption."[48] If in Heaven we are permeated with divine love, then an inspired celibate can manifest something of that divine flame in his or her devotion to Jesus.

So St. John Paul II gives helpful handles on what constitutes authentic celibacy.

First, it must be both a personal choice and a discernible "grace."[49] No pressure—the person choosing celibacy *wants* it, and

---

[47] John Paul II, *Man and Woman He Created Them*, 75:1.
[48] Ibid., 77:3-4.
[49] Ibid., 73:4.

he or she has evidence that God has given him or her the extraordinary grace to live it out.

Secondly, whoever chooses celibacy for the Kingdom's sake must also have experienced normal development in his or her masculine or feminine self; he or she has integrated the generative power of mother or fatherhood, albeit spiritual[50]—a holy longing to bless and build up a host of sons and daughters in the Spirit. One must first wrestle with the good of one's gendered longings in order to renounce physical marriage. St. John Paul II is solid here—one cannot give up what one does not desire.[51] Jesus asks for a mature choice on the part of those called to this extraordinary expression of heavenly intimacy on earth.

This discussion of inspired celibacy as another icon of Heaven helped clarify an uneasiness I have felt with some persons I've known who, because of interior sexual conflicts, disqualified themselves from marriage, using "celibacy" as a justification. Some did so because of same-sex attraction. Unmotivated to become "one flesh," they assumed a "calling" to be "one spirit" with God. St. John Paul II does not give one that "out." I interpret him in the Theology of the Body as insisting that we own our gendered selves and work out our issues out with friends and potential partners *unless and until* God gives evidence of this celibate "grace." It is a gift, not a concession to one's disintegration. So, in the meantime, one does well to work out one's conflicts and not hide them behind the collar or the veil.

Clearly, the celibate priesthood can conceal a host of conflicts that, in the worst-case scenario, can result in destruction for all involved. How much better to realize *first* the good of one's gendered

[50] Ibid., 78:5.
[51] Ibid., 81:2.

sexuality and one's capacity to be a good gift! The Theology of the Body gives one ample room to dig deeply for the true self that lies beneath ambivalence to one's own gender or the other: it is the honest, best self that Jesus unearths from the fetters of sin.

St. John Paul II frames a psychologically and spiritually robust vision for becoming a mature expression of the *gift*—the Theology of the Body invites one to consider marriage or celibacy from that vantage point. St. John Paul II wants to ensure that the gift of self, whether pledged uniquely to God or to a spouse, is done with the eyes of the heart wide open. In the Theology of the Body, the spousal meaning of the body is both the fruit of redemption and its effect; to be the gift you were meant to be, you must seek to love God and the other well, with the whole of your being.

The amazing three-part section on the words of Christ—Matthew 19 ("In the beginning"), Matthew 5 (adultery of the heart)—and Matthew 22 (resurrection of the body) prepares us for St. John Paul II's nearly rhapsodic take on Ephesians 5:21–33 and the new meaning with which Jesus endows marriage.

Simply put, marriage as a witness of Jesus' love for His Church becomes something enormous—the fusing of God's desire to wed Himself to us with the sexual love of marriage. Becoming *one flesh* reveals spiritual union, the eternal consummation we all await.

Really? Can we hear Heaven's song in the moans from the wedding bed? St. John Paul II's earthy, wholly sacramental take on marriage astounded this evangelical. God's commitment in Christ to unite Himself eternally with humanity is revealed through conjugal union.

In this I hear the Hallelujah Chorus.

Christopher West likens marriage to the trailhead that points to and leads us to the summit—the wedding feast of the Lamb. St. John Paul II goes so far as to elevate sacramental marriage to the "foundation of the whole sacramental order,"[52] in that man and woman in conjugal union make God's plan of love historical and actual—a living, groaning revelation of the deepest ache of every human heart. Contrary to Freud, that ache is for God, not for a mere body.

And yet marriage deepens and elevates the meaning of our bodies, making them heavenly vessels, not *in spite of* sexual passion but *through* it. In assuming flesh as a child, the incarnate Jesus renders our bodies capable of the holy too. He sealed that intention when He assumed our sinful flesh on the Cross.

Here was another mindblower. Marriage at once fuses these two purposes: God's *creative* and *redemptive* will for us. Not only does marriage take us "back to the beginning," but it plays it forward to the redemption of all living. Utterly powerful, this sacramental marriage.[53] The covenant that was broken between God and humanity is now renewed; it is revealed in this bodily pledge of one man for one woman. Sexual love manifests a mystery beyond itself but also activates this grace of redemption to both parties and to all who surround them.

Of course, St. John Paul II preps us for all this with a nuanced take on Ephesians 5:21-33. Sacramental marriage is more than fusing bodies—it involves both parties emulating the self-giving of Jesus and our efforts to respond to Him.[54] Simply put, in our self-giving, we try to dignify one another as Jesus has dignified each of us who open to Him.

I love how St. John Paul II builds his case for tender, attentive marital love on Ephesians 5:21: "Submit to one another out of reverence for Christ." Utterly beautiful—we discover the real form

52 Ibid., 95b:7.
53 Ibid., 97:2.
54 Ibid., 90:1-4.

of our gendered gift out of bowing low to Him; we arise in our differences, wholly equal and yet humbled by His generous love and attentive to the needs of this other. Leading out in that Spirit, men cannot get away with domination games, and women need not bristle at the call to submit indiscriminately.

——

The Theology of the Body's take on marital love resonated with my experience with Annette. For all of its imperfections, our marriage had a backbone of *agape* love that lent form and stability to the mercurial nature of erotic love. Maybe it was because sexual energies were, at first, muted for us: me because of limited experience and exposure to a woman's body, and Annette due to her sexual abuse history, which alienated her a bit from her own body.

So the fireworks built slowly. We had a mutual attraction, but in our awkwardness, we did not grope first and then talk later. We did not fall in love; we grew in love, and, as we did, our attraction to each other developed. God used our wounding for the good. Submitting to each other out of reverence meant cultivating an appreciation for the other's gendered gift without lunging after ungrounded sensations.

Too much of my young adult life had been squandered on "sensations." I had to sober up and learn to open my heart and mouth—not my pants—to persons of interest. Annette was an amazing woman to me, and I grew to love how she looked and how she cared, how she delighted in other friends and in me; I was in awe of how a woman responds to Jesus and His Spirit, how His presence lights her from within. I submitted to her wisdom, and she submitted to the direction God was leading me in ministering to persons with sexual problems. She made me and the work better.

Nothing prepared me for our honeymoon. We spent the first night at the Beverly Hills Hotel, and we loved each other with our bodies in a way that I can only say was heavenly. God's creative and redemptive will for us was realized that night. It was sensational. I love how St. John Paul II describes the language of the body—how in conjugal love our bodies prophesy of God's love for humanity, Christ's love for the Church.[55] We become a sign in the flesh of this greater reality.

Having laid a solid foundation in knowing each other with our clothes on, we were ready to let our bodies take us where words fail. Just like when we see Him face-to-face. For Heaven, I prepare no speech. We shall be overcome by love. Marital love opens me to that encounter. I love West's words: "Our bodies are Bibles." My masculine bodily love for Annette reveals good news—how He made us, how He redeems us, how He delights in fulfilling us and making us fruitful.

Children came quickly for us, and we were ready for them. Annette and I did not have any more time or money than the next guy (grad school, part-time church salary, etc.) but we loved each other wholly. Together, we could shoulder the fruit of our love. Parenting freed us to draw upon the essentially feminine and masculine aspects of our beings that, when submitted to each other, became rich resources for our kids. Simply put, Annette loved like a warm comforter; I shook out that comforter and bounced the kids up and down upon it. From us, they secured steady and empowering love. We agreed with good Pope St. Paul VI: conjugal love is at once unitive and procreative. We frustrate our own gift-giving

[55] Ibid., 23:4.

when we separate the unitive from the procreative dimensions of conjugal love.

Marriage, Annette, children, and Jesus: all invited me into the redemption of the body by making it faithful and fruitful. Having glimpsed "nakedness without shame," I was freed to forgo any residual tendency to mistrust the human body—to categorize it as bad "flesh" in opposition to the good "spirit." Chastity is all about unifying body and spirit under God to dignify our fellow humanity.

We as persons are bodies,[56] and marriage and family invited me to embrace the dignity of my self-gift and Annette's. Alive to her good (and wearied by four small children), I could keep in check the lustful, reductive aspects of my sexuality, be they expressed in using her for my own pleasure or escaping into self-pleasure. Real connection is better than the counterfeit. My body had become an instrument of love—together, through our bodies, Annette and I "made visible what is invisible, the spiritual and divine."[57] I gave to her in the spirit of Jesus, and she responded, a beautiful bride.

———

Marital chastity, as described in *Humanae Vitae* and elaborated upon in the Theology of the Body, helped me a great deal. It lifted sexuality from the merely sensational into an art—how we can cultivate an appreciation of the other without such regard needing to result in sex itself.

Obviously, this restraint does grant one the freedom to love without conceiving new life. But in the Theology of the Body, St. John Paul II takes marital chastity one step further. "It frees us to become more sensitive to the deeper and more mature values

---

[56] Ibid., 104.
[57] Ibid., 121.

connected with the spousal meaning of the body and the true freedom of the gift."[58]

Such restraint can liberate "affective manifestations" for the other that have a more pure, less selfish quality. If one thinks of lust as having a grasping "gotta-have-it" quality, then marital chastity refines lust by inviting both parties to slow down, cool off, and explore the richness of the other's gender gift that surrounds, precedes, and extends beyond genital communion. In truth, the dignity of conjugal love lies in cultivating an emotional appreciation for the other's self-gift. Marital chastity liberates this cultivation.

For St. John Paul II, the reverence in Ephesians 5:21 — mutual submission out of reverence for Christ — is a gift of the Holy Spirit. We are weak, but One who is greater helps us in our weakness to revere and not reduce the other. The Holy Spirit of self-control does just that — rather than using another, one can wait for physical release for a time that aligns with wise family planning. In the meantime, "reverencing" cultivates "a deep orientation to the personal dignity of what is intrinsically masculine and feminine" in the other. Reverencing also frees the two to honor the "dignity of the new life created by the union" when that time comes.[59]

Clearly, self-control is crucial to unifying the *unitive* aspects of marriage with the *procreative*. While the Theology of the Body humanizes openness to children in conjugal love, it accomplishes so much more. It provides a thorough vision of what it means to be human, made in God's image.

We are called, whether single or married, to reverence the other out of submission to Jesus. That means that every man has the responsibility to dignify woman, every woman the responsibility

[58] Ibid., 128:3.
[59] Ibid., 128:4.

to dignify man. Our common duality demands it. We possess the power to confirm or to conceal the other's giftedness. The Holy Spirit helps us here, empowering us when we fade or falter at confirming the good and restraining us when we are tempted to use the other for selfish purposes.

Marriage is the primary way I experience such reverence; I also do so in myriad ways as a father to my own children and to a host of spiritual children. Despite historic lust (same-sex attraction), I am grateful for the redeeming power of Jesus, who took me back to the beginning and now frees me to live like a tempered gift for others. I have the authority to love well—to seek to expand, not reduce, the horizon of another's humanity.

St. John Paul II's Theology of the Body helped clarify the good of my masculine sexuality: in spite of its imperfection, I can direct it purposefully in friendship and, most of all, in marriage. I am more fruitful in virtue than infectious in lust. In truth, through the amazing woman I married, I become more whole, as does she. We submit to each other out of reverence for Jesus—but also out of respect for one another and a host of persons who rely upon our fidelity.

Lust is no match for the Lamb who gave Himself up for me that I might love others in a way that dignifies them. I still marvel at the gift of our marriage, how Annette and I together point to where all of us are headed—the wedding feast of the Lamb. I want our self-giving to help as many as possible to prepare for that day.

Well, you may say, this is all fine for *you*. But obviously you have self-control. I don't. How am I going to direct my sexuality purposefully? Where am I going to get that self-control?

The answer is in a virtue that's so out of fashion even its name sounds old-fashioned. What you need is to understand the virtue of *prudence*.

SEVEN

Prudence and Integration

A Polish nun taught me all I need to know about prudence:

> Virtue without prudence is not virtue at all. We should often pray to the Holy Spirit for this grace of prudence. Prudence consists in discretion, rational reflection and courageous resolution. The final decision is always up to us. We must decide; we can and ought to seek advice and light.[60]

It sounds very simple. But, as St. Faustina says, we have to pray for prudence. It's not just a virtue—it's a grace.

Clear thinking about prudence was part of what eventually brought me into the Catholic Church.

While deepening my sexual ethics and ethos, the Theology of the Body drew me into the historic Church. In that way, wise

[60] Kowalska, *Divine Mercy in My Soul*, no. 1106.

and winsome mediators like Christopher West fulfilled the new evangelization of St. John Paul II. Solid instruction as to what it means to be human is good news to the searching heart.

The Theology of the Body also provided a framework for robust gift-giving: man-to-woman and woman-to-man. St. John Paul II applied chastity to married life tangibly; his work helped me to grasp how the value of my offering to Annette depended on how much it enhanced her—whether it secured her in love or destabilized her. I don't often hit the target, but when I do—there's nothing better. I am not sure that a man experiences respect more profoundly than when he gets it from the woman who knows him best and who blesses him for loving her well.

In that way, my history of same-sex attraction did not determine my personhood or my self-gift. What did determine them was the decision I made before God, and still make daily with God, to grow in love with a particular woman who knew me better than I knew myself. She never saw me as "gay" or morally disabled. Her very essence as woman invited me to exercise dimensions of my gender that might have lain dormant otherwise. Forty years later, I've integrated the role I was meant for fairly well—I'm aware of what she needs from me, while I welcome the benefits of her care. But that integration is still imperfect. We both still need God's grace to keep us clear in love.

Today, our mutual submission is seasoned and generous, especially to our grown children and their children.

Our story flies in the face of popular wisdom. Much is made today about LGBT+ "selves," which essentially amount to identities based on the ever-fracturing ground of distorted longings and self-perceptions. I would much rather invest in a "self" based upon truth, something objective on which feelings might mature.

For this, I am indebted to Fr. John Harvey, the founding leader of Courage, which ministers to Catholic persons and families impacted by same-sex attraction. Courage was founded in 1980 – the same year as Desert Stream Ministries.[61] I always valued Fr. Harvey's even-handed clarity on how humanity is ordered and on the kindness of Jesus through His members to restore the disordered. Fr. Harvey did this, not by ceding to "queer" culture, but by integrating persons into a corporate quest for chastity.

I met Fr. Harvey when I was an evangelical minister. Despite our differences, he never dismissed my offering but rather sought to bless and highlight the good he discerned.

I did push the envelope a little at Courage. Asked by Fr. Harvey to address their annual conference in the late nineties, I focused on the call of Jesus to all persons to take seriously our need to work out our humanity together as male and female. Many there assumed that same-sex attraction disqualified them from the dance of complementarity and took offense. I reasoned: either we yield our desires and self-perceptions to the One who made us in His image, or we cede to any number of selves founded in our own image. Fr. Harvey aligned with that, though he may have been more cautious about change for strugglers than I was.

He remained a friend through the years. In 2010, I sought him out in a Salesian rest home, where he died a few months later. I loved the couple of days we had together. Well into his nineties, he demonstrated a sharp mind (he was intent on completing a lecture on the difference between Alcoholics Anonymous and the Courage version of the twelve steps) and a kind heart. When I asked him outright if the problems I was already encountering in

---

[61] Desert Stream Ministries is the author's ministry, which is the source of Living Waters groups throughout the world.

my pre-Catholic considerations were worth navigating, he replied with a sparkle: "O, many troubles ahead, all worth it for this wonderful Church." He never stopped bearing the beauty and brokenness of this Body he loved.

Fr. Harvey was succeeded by Fr. Paul Check, an ace moral theologian and a generous, loving priest. Fr. Paul came alongside me and imparted wisdom and encouragement that made a way for me in the tough early days of my Catholic conversion. Somehow, he brought his moral formation to me in a way that refined, not crushed me, while honoring this new convert by requesting input on a range of pastoral questions he faced in his new post. I love him dearly. To this day, he helps me to think a little more like a moral theologian.

I am indebted to Fr. Paul for urging me to devour *The Four Cardinal Virtues* by Dr. Josef Pieper.[62] I knew of this philosopher through Leanne Payne, who late in her life urged me also to study Dr. J. Budziszewski, another philosopher whose eloquent work on natural law dovetailed with Pieper, especially in highlighting prudence. These two men cite prudence as the cardinal virtue that governs all others. Why? All other virtues must be based on what *is*. Prudence is the virtue that tells us what we can know and how we can act according to the true nature of reality.

Prudence rightly ordered my understanding and growth in chastity.

There are traditionally four cardinal virtues ("cardinal" meaning "most important"): prudence, justice, fortitude, and temperance. Prudence

---

[62] Josef Pieper, *The Four Cardinal Virtues* (San Diego: Harcourt, Brace & World, Inc., 1965).

is the one that makes the others possible. Prudence orders everything, actually. It shows us "the thing itself," the objective reality of being. Prudence directs our will and our action toward objective reality. It keeps us in the truth of things.[63] The other three cardinal virtues—justice, fortitude, and temperance—derive their goodness from prudence, for "what is good must first have been prudent."[64] One can only be just, persevering, and self-controlled if one is first prudent.

That is true because truth itself exists. The universe isn't just what you or I think of it. There is a binding reality in the universe based on God, His Being, from which comes Truth, which begets the Good.[65] And prudence, the kingpin virtue, directs our wills and our actions toward this good. We can know the good and act on it. Once we know it, we *have* to act on it. Prudence does not give us a "pass" between knowing and doing; it directs us to behold the good and somehow, prudently, to *realize* it. The prudent person turns knowledge of the truth into a decision for this truth.

J. Budziszewski anchors truth in the moral law written on our hearts, which St. Paul writes about in Romans 2:15, when he says that the Gentiles "show that the requirements of the law are written on their hearts, their consciences also bearing witness." In other words, each person—regardless of faith or lack thereof—possesses some inner sense of right and wrong. "Deep conscience, or synderesis, is the interior witness to the foundational principles of moral law."[66]

Budziszewski contrasts deep conscience, which "cannot be erased, cannot be mistaken, and is the same in every human

---

[63] Ibid., 9.
[64] Ibid., 7.
[65] Ibid., 3-4.
[66] J. Budziszewski, *What We Can't Not Know* (Dallas: Spence Publishing Company, 2003), 79.

being,"[67] with surface conscience, or *conscientia*, which is conscious moral belief, which we derive from deep conscience. On this surface level, he says, we can deceive ourselves, yet we do not lose awareness that we are in the wrong. What we "know" is knowledge, not feeling. We can thus know our wrongdoing and still feel nothing—"having lost all sensitivity," in the words of St. Paul (Eph. 4:19). In that way, "Guilty knowledge darkly asserts itself regardless of the state of feelings."[68] Thus, we can stop feeling guilty over things we still know are wrong. "A law was written on the heart of man but it was everywhere entangled with the evasions and subterfuges of men."[69]

I have come to a clear understanding of God's design for men and women through this witness of "deep conscience." Coming out of my own evasions and subterfuges as a young man compelled by same-gender lust, I began to see reality a little differently. Before I could act on it, I had to see it!

In the early days of my seeking Jesus with other young adults in Southern California, I could barely see past my still-hazy pornographic imagination. Still, I persisted to overcome the bad and pursue the true.

As I raised my hands to praise this unseen God one Sunday morning, I beheld in a young couple something true and real and right. They were seated in front of me; he offered her whatever wipes or bottle or shiny toy their baby needed, and she, composed, sought to compose the little one. Memories of my chemically altered quest for connection fell before this witness of healthy sexuality, something beautiful and ordered that corresponded to a truth in my own heart that had not been destroyed. My *feelings* did

[67] Ibid., 80.
[68] Ibid., 81.
[69] Ibid., 4.

not change—I did not desire the woman or marriage or anything at that time. I just saw reality for what it was.

It reminded me of a story I'd read years earlier. C. S. Lewis wrote a trilogy of space novels in which his hero, whose very symbolic name is Ransom, finds that other planets in our solar system are inhabited. In *Perelandra*, Ransom visits Venus and finds it to be an Eden-like paradise with a still-unfallen Adam and Eve. Faced with the beauty of innocence, he cries out in astonishment: " 'Do not move away, do not raise me up,' he said; 'I have never before seen a man or a woman. I have lived all my life among shadows and broken images.' "[70]

That was how I felt when that young family confronted me with the reality of human sexual being. For the first time, I really saw man and woman as they are.

Desires can align with truth, or they can break us, casting us into shadowlands. We make much of our desires today. If I *feel* something, I am somehow obliged to realize it, no matter how disordered those desires may be or how fruitless the end of pursuing those desires may be.

Natural law says no.

———

What is natural law? Simply put, natural law is the understanding that certain truths don't depend on us. There is a real standard of morality. There are principles of human action that we can understand by understanding the truth of how and why we were created.

In his reflection on natural law, Budziszewski points us not to desires but to design. Regardless of our feelings, we are "God's canvas"—we actually possess a human nature that may be a little

[70] C. S. Lewis, *Perelandra* (New York: Scribner, 1996), 176.

lost to us, but it still remains and can be summoned in blessed moments, like that glimpse of family that one Sunday morning that resonated in my depths.

We seem to have lost our grasp of what "natural" means. Today, we use it in terms of what seems right to *me*, whatever I feel or desire. "Homosexuality is natural for me, heterosexuality for you" — that's the attitude popular culture teaches us. Budziszewski is clear that "a natural inclination is not whatever I desire; it is not even what everybody desires. The point of the adjective 'natural' is to point to design."[71]

Design figures big in my friend and scholar Dr. Robert Gagnon's definitive book on what Scripture says about homosexuality, *The Bible and Homosexual Practice*.[72] His fundamental premise hinges upon design. He emphasizes "the revelatory authority of Scripture, combined with the witness of nature, to which the Bible points, that is, the complementarity of male and female sexual organs as the most unambiguous clue people have of God's intent for gender pairing."[73] The description of gender origins in Genesis 1–3 provides justification for the physical, interpersonal, and procreative sexual complementarity of male and female, which "will reappear as a continuous thread in the Old Testament, early Jewish, and New Testament critiques of same-sex intercourse as 'contrary to nature.'"[74]

Gagnon's mastery of ancient languages, and his familiarity with historic documents written alongside Scripture, strengthens his premise that homosexual activity violates God's beautiful design

---

[71] Budziszewski, *What We Can't Not Know*, 106.

[72] Robert A. J. Gagnon, *The Bible and Homosexual Practice: Texts and Hermeneutics* (Nashville: Abingdon Press, 2001).

[73] Ibid., 41.

[74] Ibid., 62.

for humanity and incurs what can only be described in Scripture as His intense disfavor. Gagnon makes an airtight case that "same-sex intercourse constitutes an inexcusable rebellion against the intentional design of the created order."[75]

Hard, true stuff.

Yet the hard truth of God's design and its relevance for all, even those with feelings to the contrary, can be an invitation. Choosing to see myself as a part of this design—man for woman, woman for man—was the beginning of freedom for me. As Annette and I progressed in our friendship, I grew attuned to her whole being, body and spirit—I could read her joy and frustration, and I comprehended her need for me and my longing to unite myself with her. Over time, I longed to close the gap between us and to experience the goodness of our becoming one. There was a shift in our side-by-side friendship when I realized that I wanted unity, oneness, and body-to-body communion with Annette. It was knowledge (this is the woman for me) and desire (I want her). Prudence required walking together with our clothes on long before consummation, but we journeyed together toward that end.

I love that awakening, a combination of clear seeing, or knowing, plus the desire to will and to act responsibly upon what one sees and knows. Here we see prudence at work, "that the good may be loved and made reality";[76] I sought with my eyes wide open to love a real, imperfect person. Prudence helped me here, to know her as best I could and to love her as best as I could. Prudence must line up with reality!

[75] Ibid., 37.
[76] Pieper, *The Four Cardinal Virtues*, 24.

Unlike the powerful "gay" feelings that compelled me and my male friends to partake of each other sexually without any value of fidelity, I acted upon prudent love and reserved sexual love for one person, whose very difference from me drew me into a deepening awareness of who she was. Sexual encounters confirmed that quest and provoked both will and desire to know her more. Pieper speaks of the power of sensual impulses "to split the power of decision in two,"[77] rendering one imprudent and divided in one's grasp of reality. I had to walk through a lot of tempting experiences with guys in order to discover that I could choose enduring love for a whole person, rather than fracture myself and another for a sensational moment or two.

Reality makes me happy; I thrive when acting upon my true nature. Pope Emeritus Benedict XVI underscores this when he says: "Man too has a nature that he must respect and that he cannot manipulate at will. Man is not merely self-creating freedom. Man does not create himself. He is intellect and will, but he is also nature, and his will is rightly ordered if he respects his nature, listens to it and accepts himself for who he is, as one who did not create himself. In this way, and in no other, is true human freedom fulfilled."[78] I am a man endowed with a spiritual and physical essence to love a woman well. I may falter at this for a variety of reasons, but my failings neither change my nature nor alter the inspired trajectory of learning how to offer myself well according to that nature. My freedom is bound up in this love: spiritually, anthropologically, and psychologically.

I may at times strain, like all fallen creatures who endure their shame for the joy set before them, but it is true aspiration and real

[77] Ibid., 19.
[78] Pope Benedict XVI, Address of His Holiness Benedict XVI: Reichstag Building, Berlin (September 22, 2011).

joy. I choose to operate in reality. I have no other self, no other nature than the one made in the image of Him who has aligned Himself with the call to love his counterpart well. Thus, to the twenty-first century western citizen who declares that his or her truest self is "gay" or "lesbian" or "trans" or "bi," I say: "Thank you for sharing your innermost feelings; please be assured that I see you, not as the sum of your sexual feelings, but as a man or woman made in God's image."

LGBT+ persons exist only in their own fallen imaginations. Perhaps our Creator and Redeemer sees instead persons wounded by abuse and neglect who have come to mistake emotional needs for erotic ones, persons snagged by sexualized same-gender friendships or seduced by rejection of their own anatomy, persons yet to resume the journey to reality by making peace with their sexuality and their need for the other gender. This reality corresponds with our inspired nature, from which we grow in human freedom as we learn to act prudently.

I am grateful for a host of men and women in whom I see the evidence of such prudence. Dan Mattson, the author of *Why I Don't Call Myself Gay*, writes compellingly of how his return to the Catholic faith as a man with same-sex attraction radically shifted his self-definition from "gay" to a chaste son of the Father.[79] His witness as a progressively integrated single man, decried by the LGBT+ community, blazes a trail for thousands seeking reality in their identities.

I cannot underestimate the importance of his message. Increasingly, a host of young persons who came of age in the last decade

[79] Daniel C. Mattson, *Why I Don't Call Myself Gay: How I Reclaimed My Sexual Reality and Found Peace* (San Francisco: Ignatius Press, 2017).

are being tossed about by false definitions that strengthen their gender disintegration. And well-meaning but ill-informed caregivers are conferring these misbegotten selves upon them as if teen fragility can only be guarded with a lie! It is much better to tell young people the truth.

Raised Catholic, my friend Kelsie suffered early exposure to all kinds of porn and sex play, encouraging her reliance on female sensuality as a way of feeling protected and affirmed. During her senior year of high school, a slightly older woman seduced her and then dropped her soon after; Kelsie staggered into a Catholic retreat, where she met a prudent, merciful priest. He helped her to exchange her sins for forgiveness and the new and true self conferred on her by the Father. Many years and steps later, she has learned to walk in that self beautifully. Again, feelings don't define the reality of who we are. God does.

My friend Jonathan Hunter discovered the same, and he continues to act prudently. He was among the first wave of young Americans in the late sixties who were baptized as members of a "queer" nation. He was privileged—a handsome and gifted artist who recalls the spiritual darkness that shrouded him when he "came out" as a "gay" man and began defining himself as such. "It was as if a wall fell around me and I knew I was trapped by my own self-definition. My fate was sealed. No more becoming."

Then a drug overdose and an experience of God's merciful presence woke him up and compelled him to seek Jesus. Jonathan discovered a small band of faithful God-seekers and, together with them, made every effort to align his whole being with Jesus. He began to identify with Jesus and forsook his "gay" identity; he grew quickly as a son of the Father and made peace with the solid man he aspired to become. Jonathan discovered he was HIV positive, which only hastened his aspiration to offer himself chastely to both men and women. Nearly forty years ago, he received the call to serve brothers and sisters with HIV. He gets stronger with time. Annette and I agree wryly that Jonathan will outlive us all. Another friend, Peter, leads a group in Manhattan for men and women coming out of homosexuality. Members attend churches throughout the city, and I am constantly amazed at the fruit of his labor. The Father meets the faithful there, opens their eyes to reality, and in many cases equips them for marriage. As I experienced with Annette, there is something virginal about these redemption stories, as if we, along with Ransom and others, are seeing Eden for the first time. Greg, one of Peter's members, shared this with us:

I love being married. We're only two weeks into it, but it's absolutely wonderful.

For those of us on the journey out of same-sex attraction, we tend to emphasize healthy friendships with other men. But I must say, being married has helped me to understand and embrace my masculinity as nothing else has.

There was a moment when my wife and I happened to be standing near each other in front of a nearly full-length mirror, naked. Just seeing the male and female bodies next to each other—our bodies—I suddenly understood the beauty and wonder of the differences between the genders. Mine is angular, strong, and defined; hers is gentle, soft, and inviting. They make sense only in that mine was created for her and hers for me, to be given to each other as a gift.

As far as physical union in marriage, I am most definitely heterosexual ... one thing that has pleasantly surprised me is that, although I have always been physically attracted to my wife, I am more filled with awe and wonder at the beauty of her body with each passing day. There is something glorious about the feminine body as God created it, something especially glorious when it is a precious gift given to you (and only you) by the person you love most in the world. Her body is beautiful, just as a sunset is beautiful, or an undiscovered land lit by the morning light. I look at her, catch my breath, and wonder how God could be so good as to give her to me.

Reality. The grace to perceive reality correctly and to act on it. Especially in the sexual realm, prudence matters; in our fallen selves, today's glimpse of Eden in the other can become tomorrow's temptation in the wilderness. For this, we need prudence and her steadying hand to guard our knowledge of things as they really are and to make wise decisions constantly that line up with that knowledge. These choices need to be made "with energetic promptness" so that, in the heat or boredom of the moment, we can stay true to reality and continue in happy self-giving.

I would also broaden our understanding here to include persons who are discerning or living out a celibate calling for the sake of the Kingdom.

For married men like Greg and me, the measure of love's prudence is tested by an actual person, a spouse. For the celibate, this "measure" may not be as clear. Given the new and understandable scrutiny celibate ministers face today, prudence may help ascertain the veracity of such a call.

I had the privilege of walking with our friend Jonathan Hunter—the one who had overcome drugs and HIV—as we, the community around him, helped him discern his calling as a celibate evangelical minister. We, as his ministry family, witnessed grace-filled earmarks of chastity in his life; we could also behold his unique bond with Jesus, who appeared to be directing and enabling him to carry out a particular mission. Our long journey with Jonathan granted us the confidence to lay hands on him in agreement with his pledge to celibacy before both God and his fellows.

Discerning celibacy has special challenges for people like Jonathan and others who have histories of same-sex attraction. Prudent decisions must be made based on reality. One cannot just assume that one's same-sex attraction disqualifies one from the prospect of wholly relating to the opposite gender and that therefore one is called to celibacy. It's essential to look deeply at one's same-sex attraction and discern what is going on at the core of these desires.

The parallels between marriage and the unique call to celibacy have become increasingly clear to me. If I as a man am discerning marriage to a woman, I must look at whether the whole of *me* desires the whole of *her*. It requires challenge and doubt, but also self-awareness as to how she, unlike anyone else, is the one for me. I would repent quickly of any tendency to use her as a cover for my broken sexuality—to employ marriage to camouflage underlying conflicts. That possibility must be exposed and refused in order to reveal whether my yes to her is based on the desire to offer myself to her in a bond of love. It would necessitate counsel from the community and clear communication between us. She needs to know me—all of me—and I need to know her in the light of where I have come from in my disorder, where I am going in my seasoned commitment to chastity, and how we can go forward together, in real self-giving—weaknesses and wonders combined.

Similarly, a person seeking Jesus in a kind of spousal partnership while fulfilling a particular mission must demonstrate over time that he or she is not using a spiritual vocation as a cover for poor human relationships. How many teens historically have gravitated to the priesthood due to shame over same-sex attraction, leading them to conclude that a spiritual vocation may be the best way to resolve what appears to be a dead-ended sexual future? And tragically, how many similarly disintegrated priests and bishops have heard such teens' garbled confessions and have groomed them for a religious life that may well have included unchaste bonds forged in the all-male community of seminary and beyond?

Clearly, we need to give more time and energy to help candidates for celibate vocations discover themselves before God as human beings with desires, conflicts, and hard choices to make. Might the love of reality—our beautiful Creator endowing His creature with the longing to create—shine upon what may be deep, shameful divides in His chosen ones?

Understanding these divides is all the more important in the Internet age.

———

We can say without a doubt that a global virtual porn superhighway has defiled most young people's imaginations, including the religious. Clutching the cell phone like an idol, a generation has fused with sexual excess. For some, this is a poor substitute for relating to real members of the opposite gender. To others, it introduces addiction to sexualizing one's own gender. This tempts the unwary to mistake lust for his or her need to take basic pre-sexual steps in the direction of gender integration.

In my experience, porn is more of a temptation for persons in shame over their same-sex attraction than it is for the average opposite-gender idolater. Unwilling to commit the felony of same-sex behavior, the soon-to-be addict stokes the impulse in the misdemeanor of massive "gay" porn use. This utterly scrambles reality and empowers the faulty notion that one is an intrinsic, high-octane "homosexual."

Here, lust confuses the decision. Instead of embarking on the good, hard work of looking at one's sexual divides and working out a plan to emerge out of the domination of same-sex attraction and into a whole-enough gendered self, one settles. In a world that confirms the lie that you were "born that way," and that energy spent "changing" is in vain and hazardous to one's health, it's easy to align with the LGBT+ mantra "I am 'gay' and you just have to be okay with that."

I am indebted here to the work of Drs. Kleponis and Fitzgibbons and their article: "The Distinction between Deep-Seated Homosexual Tendencies and Transitory Same-Sex Attractions in Candidates for Seminary and Religious Life."[80] These experts help persons discern whether or not they are good candidates for the Catholic priesthood or religious life. They describe men who view their homosexuality as inborn, the basis for their sexual identification, and possess no interest in looking more deeply at any emotional or relational conflicts that may have contributed to their same-sex attraction. In other words, these men regard their sexual attractions as not disordered and themselves in no need of "reordering."

Unwilling to reframe their same-sex attraction, these candidates are described by the good doctors as possessing deep-seated homosexual tendencies and as being vulnerable to a "significant affective immaturity with excessive anger and jealousy toward males who are not homosexual. Their insecurity leads them to

---

[80] Peter C. Kleponis and Richard P. Fitzgibbons, "The Distinction between Deep-Seated Homosexual Tendencies and Transitory Same-Sex Attractions in Candidates for Seminary and Religious Life," *The Linacre Quarterly*, November 29, 2013, https://www.tandfonline.com/doi/pdf/10.1179/002436311803888302.

avoid close friendship with men who do not have SSA [same-sex attraction]."[81] Clearly, such persons are interpreting their same-sex attraction in a way that prevents much if any movement toward their true natures.

On the other hand, Kleponis and Fitzgibbons are hopeful for those who take a good, hard look at their lives and commit to a process of healing and moral formation that will enable them to emerge into whole-enough persons. I am working with one such young man—Mike—who was referred by one of his seminary formation guides to a week-long healing and training week we offer. There he became aware of a quiet agreement that he had made between his same-sex attraction and a perceived disqualification from "normal" married life. Loving Jesus much, he opted for priestly formation and, prior to meeting us, had never taken a good, hard look as to whether he was capable of a life outside of the celibate priesthood.

He is taking a break from seminary now and discovering the "world of women" (in no improper way) as a man created for a woman. He is realizing that before he can refuse natural fathering, he must first enter the dance of male/female relating. He must know what he is renouncing! That includes, but extends far beyond, sexual arousal; it means putting himself "out there" with real women and discovering who they are and who he is as a man called to live in co-humanity with them, whether as a clergyman or as a husband. We're not sure which yet, but Mike is clear on one thing: he is refusing the reality-denying assumption that a history of same-sex feelings is life-defining and inclines him to a priestly calling. He wants the Father's will for his fathering so that his yes can be yes, be it in marriage or in the priesthood.

---

[81] Ibid., 357.

By his own will to align with reality, Mike embodies what Kleponis and Fitzgibbons cite as a man with "transitory same-sex attractions": men "who do not base their masculine identity upon their sexual attractions ... they do not believe that they were born with [these attractions] and greatly desire to overcome them.... They accept the fullness of the Church's teaching on sexual morality and want to live and teach it. They do not ascribe to current societal views on homosexuality and same-sex unions. These men are highly motivated to work in psychotherapy to identify the origins of their conflicts and to resolve them."[82]

Here, prudence comes into play, as it does for anyone with sexual conflicts who wills to decide maturely how to act—be it in marriage, singleness, or any ministry demanding celibacy. I love how Pieper unites Spirit-inspired prudence—the gift God gives us to help us become prudent—and the goal of prudence, a process of developing "a naturally perfected ability." That ability involves three aspects that I shall highlight now and apply to broken persons who—graced and goaded by prudence—become chaste.

—•—

Memory is first—that is, "true-to-being memory." This is the capacity not to falsify what we recall, but rather to make sure that memory contains "real things and events as they really are and were."[83]

Chastity demands accurate recollection of our lives, neither dramatizing nor minimizing their contours.

I would apply this pointedly to the psychotherapeutic process where "deep calls to deep" and invites us to consider the suffering that inclined us to disorder. I see again and again the tendency of LGBT+

---

[82] Ibid.
[83] Pieper, *The Four Cardinal Virtues*, 15.

affirming persons to claim an Edenic childhood to make a case for a "born-that-way," "natural" tendency. This imprudent interpretation can be matched by sufferers who frame their entire childhoods as horrific and disfiguring, as if there was nothing good in their house of horrors. Both extremes are implausible and highly edited versions of reality—and both, perhaps, framed for ideological reasons.

I much prefer the prudent approach to therapy, which allows us to explore the uniqueness of each of our lives and discover that (mostly) well-intentioned persons damaged us; thin-skinned and reactive, we were capable of cultivating ideas about ourselves and others that simply were not true. Add to that the truth that our common enemy is merciless toward us, knows something about our thematic vulnerabilities, and will orchestrate events that deepen layers of confusion, self-hatred, and shame, one after another.

Therapy helped me to own some of this suffering, which I had not been able to see clearly enough or to grieve. Through prudent memory, I was able to reclaim real pain—real emotion—that had been circumvented and drowned in same-sex excess. My friend, the late Dr. Joseph Nicolosi, helped me to see how living in the awareness and expression of our suffering is among the best antidotes to lust. You cannot grieve and seek to consume another sexually at the same time! Put more bluntly, to quote one of his clients: "Now I would rather cry than masturbate."[84]

I came to understand in therapy, through prudent memory, that I hated pain and wanted to assuage it in sensual addictions. Incorporating sorrow and anger into my life was thus a hallmark of my chastity: this value contributed to prayers of lament, angry devotions, deep friendships, and an impassioned marriage.

[84] Joseph J. Nicolosi, *Shame and Attachment Loss: The Practical Work of Reparative Therapy* (Downers Grove: InterVarsity Press, 2009), 91.

Similarly, chaste memory means not reframing the immoral past through a rose-colored lens. Many of my friends had divided lives before their marriages; several were unfaithful in their marriages. In the drone or tension of real life, these friends can be tempted to look fondly at illicit love as a temporary escape clause. Prudence demands we seal those potholes. Often, they contribute to longing on the sly for lost lovers whom we summon in our imaginations to displace the real, flawed women we married.

All lies! Imagined lovers change no diapers, adore us without challenge, know all of our needs, and attend them slavishly. Then they stab us in the back by the dawn's early light, and we are left alone, miserable in our shame and cowardice. Prudence reclaims the uprightness of memory by helping us to lay aside childish things so we can get on with the business of reality: real people who need us to be present to them in love.

My friend Jim had a homosexual affair early in his marriage. It was sensational: it briefly actualized all he had fantasized about. His lover moved on, and Jim was left with only a memory and his now distraught wife. Both spouses have worked hard to reclaim the integrity of their marriage. To do so, he had to close the door — to "die" to the recollection of adultery, the "what-ifs" that remained — even if the memory brought him pleasure." When I recall the devastating truth my 'freedom' wrought, I release it to Jesus fast and look at my wife and kids. I dug a deep hole in my moral failing. I worked hard to get out of that hole. I refuse to romanticize what almost sunk my life and a few other lives too."

———

The second aspect of developing "a naturally perfected ability" of prudence is *docility*, or "open-mindedness," a spirit made bright by a porous understanding of things and experiences.[85] I like to think of such openness as involving (though not limited to) a discerning reliance upon the virtue of others—turning from pride and isolation into real, ongoing community. That alone shatters the lie that "no one can really know me as I am and love me"—perhaps the biggest lie that keeps us bound to grandiosity and self-hatred while it opens us to imprudent acts. Prudence opens the door to wise fellowship, where we, fragile in our chastity, discover that our fellows—not mere abstinence—are the solution to our addictions.

Let me give you a personal example. I had a rotten experience in a faraway land with a pastor who clearly did not like me and wished he had not invited me to his corner of the world. I felt tempted to experience this traditional man, machismo in his bearing, as a familiar rejecter of one like me, whom he perceived as soft and silly. I reflected on this demeaning experience *en route* to my departing flight, coming under a deeply felt shame response that had defined much of my childhood—set adrift, cut off, and inexplicably flawed in my masculinity. The familiar lures of alcohol and porn came up immediately, and I thought of how I might secure both.

Then I thought: "Wait a minute! I'm fifty-four, not fourteen! Now I can do something right that I didn't know how to do then." I called a beloved brother of mine who was still healing from his own addiction—and as such, he was a reliable source of divine mercy. I told him ashamedly about my weekend from Hell and the shame-marked events of my past that it elicited. He encouraged me but, most importantly, prayed that Jesus would come right into that vulnerable moment through the Holy Spirit and

85 Pieper, *The Four Cardinal Virtues*, 16.

uphold me in my dignity as His son, who did not have anything to be ashamed of! Immediately, the heaviness and accusation fell away and I was able to travel home with my integrity intact, more confident in Jesus' power to use all things for good—even to use a day-old wound to heal a forty-year-old one!

Docility invites us into the world of unexpected gifts, refinement, and empowerment through the Christ who is present in our brother or sister. We open in weakness and are surprised by the mercy and wisdom that we receive.

We discover something else, too. Even in our recovering state, we can convey to another something of the Jesus who is growing and surfacing in our own lives!

———

The third aspect of growing in prudence involves *choice*: "a perfected ability to decide for the good."[86]

That means steering life with clear-sighted objectivity in unexpected circumstances. To me, this involved discovering the interplay over time between our own responses to hardship, growing to understand the responses of those we love most, and having faith that, under the Father's gaze, we might trust our own instincts in swiftly choosing the right course of action.

Two examples might help. At the very beginning of Desert Stream Ministries, I met with a young man, roughly my age, who began to act seductively toward me as I told a little of my story and the services we offered. I was puzzled at first by his behavior, then pleased: I liked being wanted by him. Quickly, I came to my senses and decided that our meeting had gone long enough. I politely excused myself and fled. He lit a fire in me that burned

[86] Ibid.

for a couple of days. I wanted badly to connect with him again, but I knew my intentions were sexual, not pastoral.

In my struggle, I reached out to my then-fiancée, Annette; we connected and prayed, and I simmered down. Soon after, I spoke with that guy and reiterated that he was free to come to the group but needed to be clear about his sexual intentions toward members. He got that message without feeling demeaned. After all, he had every right to be a messy person—he was coming for help! *I'm* the one with the responsibility to act decisively and prudently in situations where my pure offering can get contaminated by my own weaknesses, brought to light by another. I need to see it, own it, and act. Had I not, God would have forgiven me. He could not, however, have entrusted the care of broken souls to me. God is *prudent*, and He insists that I become like Him in this virtue.

During one season of international ministry, I felt inexplicably worn down. Several domestic tensions percolated (one being my new status as a catechumen, which caused problems everywhere). I could tell Annette was suffering at the prospect of my leaving again. I told myself all the reasons that I had to go and lead a multi-national team—advertising, expectation, people who would bail if I backed out. Then, without any more deliberation, I knew I had to cancel my end of the trip and delegate all else, trusting God with the result. No negotiation, nothing. I also canceled a couple of less complicated trips and simply leaned into the person I love most, my wife, who I knew was suffering most over my pre-Catholic state. We needed to be together. Period. Prudence freed me to make a swift, essential decision for the good.

———

Prudence means loving what is good and real, and making sure decisions for this good reality. It is clear now why this virtue is the entry way into the other "cardinals"—justice, fortitude, and temperance. Clearly it has presided over the chaste aspirations of all mentioned in this chapter, including myself. Prudence has clarified the good of God's design in creating us male and female and the path toward realizing that design in a manner that invites us to rely on Jesus and His Church; I trust similarly that prudence makes us more like Him, better members of Jesus for one another.

At the end of the day, we stand before Jesus and must give an answer for what we knew and how, through grace, we acted upon that knowledge. Prudence always builds toward that end, toward the future. Perhaps those most scorched by the fires of imprudence can, in their training in prudence, exemplify how today's choices for the good build toward tomorrow. May we seek to grasp her deep meaning more fully, and may she grasp us more fully, in order that we might walk in a manner worthy of Jesus, all our days.

> My son, do not let wisdom and understanding out of your sight, preserve sound judgment and discretion; they will be life for you, an ornament to grace your neck.
> Then you will go on your way in safety, and your foot will not stumble. When you lie down, you will not be afraid; when you lie down, your sleep will be sweet. (Prov. 3:21-24)

That discernment, that prudence, keeps us in touch with the truth. Once we understand what *is*, we can begin to know what *ought to be*. That is why prudence underlies the other virtues. And the first of those other virtues is the one that tells us how what *we* need should be balanced with what *others* need. We call that virtue *justice*.

EIGHT

Justice and Integration

My friend Roger had a series of affairs during the first decade of his marriage. It was the strength of his Christian community that finally led him to confess and turn from his sins. Submitting to a team of elders, he embarked on a course of restoration.

As he became known by others, Roger discovered that his obvious sins were a symptom of a deeper problem. He suffered from narcissism—an obsession with his image. On the one hand, he loved pleasing others at church and at home as a "good" Christian. On the other hand, he was creating a seductive self in which he could slavishly adore and be adored by another sexually.

"Maybe I've never really loved anyone," he said, a symptom of his divided life.

The mercy of the elder brothers who surrounded him proved liberating. He had been locked up in himself and his own swirl of addiction and shame for decades. Now he felt free for the first time from the underlying fear that he would be exposed and disgraced. There he was: known as the worst sinner, yet deeply loved, for the first time. He rejoiced as one raised from the dead. The prodigal had returned to party with his homeboys.

His wife, Kim, did not join the celebration. Though grateful, she admitted to Roger: "I am glad you are growing in relation to Christ Resurrected. I am still stuck at the Crucifixion." That is, the still-crucifying knowledge of what he had done to her and their children. She was troubled by the new realization that maybe he did not love her and that maybe she wasn't "enough" for him and never would be. Her relief lay solely on the fact that she wasn't losing her mind; the nagging sense that something was deeply wrong in the marriage was true.

Roger struggled to see why she could not at least encourage him in his good, hard efforts. He had yet to see how devastated she was by it all and how he unintentionally had replaced a destructive self-absorption (adultery) with a constructive one (recovery).

Finally, he woke up and realized that her healing — and theirs — had just begun.

He acted prudently — saw things as they were. He needed a lot of help here. It is tough for one narcissistically inclined person to bear another's brokenness, especially when he caused the damage! Truth-telling elders mirrored mercy and justice to Roger. They implored him to endure and not cast off the burden he had placed on Kim's shoulders. With their guidance, he began the long, slow turn toward Kim's need for healing. And he made peace with the extended timeframe it would take for their marriage to heal.

That was costly. Adultery exacts a huge toll. Kim had years of questions, anger, resentment, grief, and contempt for him. She also needed healing for her lack of self-love that preceded the marriage, which was nearly destroyed by his infidelities.

Adultery cuts deep — so deep that it rips apart the two God has joined as one. Only mercy, understood rightly through the grid of real justice, can heal such a wound. Such seasoned mercy, activated by the willing participation of both spouses, gave them hope for the restoration of their marriage.

It took Kim a decade to process all of this honestly. God, friends, healers, and her husband met her in her pain. And others came alongside to help them sort out what it meant to trust each other in the present. That meant Kim made peace with her husband, who was still weak but not wicked. He had to prove himself trustworthy through reliance upon his upright band of brothers. She needed to release him to his process of healing; after all, his disorder preceded the marriage, and he had never worked it out in the light of others.

Prudence laid the foundation for restoration. But justice—giving Kim what was due to her based on what is right—stood on the shoulders of prudence and commanded a systemic approach to rectify what was wrong (his betrayal of her). God forgave Roger, but only Roger, in the truth and strength given to him by God, could serve the justice required to restore the marriage.

Justice requires a right concept of man, of human nature. We then can determine, based on this right concept, what we owe another.

For example, in the area of marriage, faithfulness to our marital vows is a right concept of man.[87] These realities must be determined objectively, according to the truth that "every external act has a social character."[88] In other words, one's moral actions always impact others. There is no such thing as a victim-free sin. Pieper writes: "No private relations between individuals exist. Man's life

---

[87] Pieper, *The Four Cardinal Virtues*, 49.
[88] Ibid., 63.

has a totally public character because the individual is adequately defined only through his membership in the social whole, which is the only reality."[89]

This "membership in the social whole" has huge implications for restoring persons (and their families) who have perpetrated sexual sins and may even feel justified in breaking boundaries.

I recall teaching at a large church where a colleague of mine had great success in gathering men who had committed adultery. These men found communion and were learning to connect humbly with each other instead of further violating their wives and their illicit lovers. However, when I asked about the wives and their healing, they looked blank. Nobody had considered the ones most in need of healing! Each wife was suffering the impact of another's sin, a violation she had not chosen. What was taken from them — trust in spousal fidelity — had a far more disruptive and disorienting quality than the adultery perpetrated willfully and deliberately by their husbands.

Of course, women are capable of adultery too, and perhaps no variety is as vexing as when a wife announces that she is hooking up with another woman. I have known good men who, typically naïve about the nature of female same-sex attraction, are flabbergasted that a good wife and mother is now claiming a "born that way" and thus "must be free to act that way" justification.

A deacon in a large parish called me distraught over his wife's lesbian affair. She had informed him about this friendship that became sexual and was now displacing the marriage. He was confused: a pastor from another parish was counseling her and advocating for her same-sex relationship. That priest made the case that she was acting on her true self and that the kindest thing the husband

---

[89] Ibid., 74.

could do was to make way for her authentic decisions. What came to mind were Dr. Robert Gagnon's words: "Few areas are so given to deception as the area of sexuality. While the potential for pleasure is the greatest, the potential for clever and self-serving sophistry is also the greatest."[90]

I told the deacon that this priest was wrong. Though his wife undoubtedly felt a profound conflict of desire, one's desires do not justify divorce and abandoning kids for a dream lover. One can still choose for the common good. In the case of marital repair, that requires a concerted effort on the part of two persons. I implored both of them to seek help together for what had become an unhappy marriage (this deacon had neglected her for work and ministry), hoping that she might begin to express the range of her needs. She agreed to see a seasoned counselor with him and to seek guidance together from another priest who had not bought into the lie that same-sex desires justify selfish and unjust behavior.

Pieper would agree. He writes prophetically: "The whole field of sexual aberration, not adultery and rape only, contains an element of injustice.... We are apt to concentrate almost exclusively on the subjective significance of dissoluteness as it affects the one who performs the act; whereas it usually escapes us that it is the order of our communal life and the realization of the common good which are equally affected."[91]

—————

From the beginning, Annette and I had to work out in our marriage how much of a threat my history of sexual brokenness was to her security as a woman. As my wife, she will always have the right to

[90] Gagnon, *The Bible and Homosexual Practice: Texts and Hermeneutics*, 41.
[91] Pieper, *The Four Cardinal Virtues*, 61.

my attraction and fidelity to her. So we had to find talking points that enabled us to sort through her fears and my struggles. I say "struggles" rather than conceding to repeated failure. The latter is not a struggle: it is giving in to one's worst impulses, as if one has no recourse. Every person, every sinner, possesses a will—we have some speck of authority that, like a mustard seed, can grow into a mighty tree if we tend to it.

Let us not make the common error of using spiritual language like a "cross to bear" or a "thorn in the flesh" to describe sinful habits. That makes noble what Jesus detests and calls us to turn from. St. Paul certainly struggled with some vexing tendency that God did not remove, but he was not a sex addict! Let's call addiction what it is—a deep, sinful habit that damages our walk with Jesus and the people we love most.

To be sure, we cannot always choose the direction of our sinful inclinations, and some desires (e.g., same-sex attraction, fetishistic desires, etc.) may be more shameful than others. We simply must divide the inclination from the sin. We can choose what we do with our inclinations. For example, we can be open about them and confess them regularly to trustworthy people when they flare up. We can seek to "read" our inclinations wisely and halt fueling them with vain fantasies. But we dare not sanctify our seductive dance with idols by making it a "cross." The Cross invites us to die to the dance. Let's stop patting ourselves on the back for wanting to dance and thinking ourselves pious for refusing pretty poisons.

Though I had temptations to porn, and at times an emotional pull to certain men, I was neither hidden nor addicted to behavioral patterns linked to these tendencies. A *tendency* is not a stronghold of moral darkness. In truth, I loved my wife on both emotional and physical levels and could say then, as I do now, that my weaknesses were not wicked.

Annette knew who I was: a man who possessed both strengths and weaknesses. And she was mature enough, even as a young woman, to know that my weaknesses preexisted our relationship. She learned what these tendencies could become — late-night television or computer stuff that digressed into unclean images, or the occasional friendship in which she rightly perceived an unnatural interest on my part. I sought to be forthcoming with her when I felt weak, and she was free to express when my emotional vacancy demanded that she ask, "Are you okay?"

I felt some shame about this, good shame I hope, but not the kind that bred a double life. I knew that my sexual fidelity to her meant living undivided in my thoughts and in my relationships. Any quiet adultery could render me impotent. Or even if it fired me up, it would be an alien fire, an unclean passion that she would discern as sourced in the father of lies, not life.

I am kind of a computer dunce so I am pretty much unable to leap over the blocks on my devices. Except once. I managed to hurdle the barrier and was so shocked that I stopped; I felt a fear of God, like I could lose sleep and sanctity and even my marriage over this slop. Before leaving on a trip that next day, Annette requested use of my phone to check the weather, and the first thing that came up was a foul image.

Ouch. (I had no idea how to delete it.) That discovery was humiliating to me and hurtful to her. It was super good that it happened — it is better to expose the idols now than to be damned by them on the Day of Judgment. It was tough for Annette, as my sin allowed the fear of infidelity into the marriage. We had to talk it through, and I had to recommit to her and to my accountability partners to rebuild the walls that were burned by my lustful action. Again, I can and will *choose* not to go there again. With a little help from my friends.

Annette has a right to know that I, in weakness, am present to Jesus and to my accountability partners. She knows, too, that we can talk about these things before they get out of hand. I have even found that a willingness to disclose the hard stuff we face in our interior lives (and Annette has her share as well) builds intimacy. At times, it functions as a kind of foreplay—light burning off shadows and mercy freeing us from fig leaves. Such nakedness can awaken pure love. I have found that freedom to share honestly and to hear one another respectfully is the basis for a solid sexual relationship.

I love this quote from a former professor of mine: "Lovemaking in its proper context involves the entire process of communication. . . . To become a successful lover is to become a person who is able to relate to your partner in the totality of your personality. To skimp or shield your partner from any part of you is to diminish your sexual relationship."[92]

Ascertaining what is going on with one's spouse in the resurfacing of old feelings and temptation to sin is essential to marital health and justice. It is also tough and shameful. Building a solid base of communication where both parties can express weakness, fears, and encouragement is essential. If we cannot hear one another without escalating into panic or digressing into lies, the marriage ceases to be a safe place for either party to tell the truth. The beginning of real justice requires reality—what is going on? What does it mean? Where is choice?

———

Communities of faith do a great service by helping couples work out their difficult sexual histories so they can face together the possibility of these past problems resurfacing during difficult seasons

[92] Dennis B. Guernsey, *Thoroughly Married* (Waco: Word Books, 1975), 28.

of married life. What matters most is that both parties are committed to giving the other their best. Each should be ready to say to the other, "I tell the truth in order not to sin against you. I seek only your best—I want my words and actions to secure you in love." In other words, the spouse committed to chastity makes a commitment to justice in marriage by making clear his or her choice to give all to this other, even if "all" is diminished by preexisting weaknesses that make the effort strenuous and at times shameful.

Pieper helps us here: "The state of equilibrium that properly corresponds to man's essence, to his original paradisiac state, is constantly thrown off balance and has constantly to be 'restored' through an act of justice.... This return to equilibrium is an unending task. That means that the dynamic character of man's communal life finds its image within the very structure of every act of justice. Restitution implies ... that is never possible for man to realize an ideal and definitive condition."[93]

Marriages must embrace the challenge of flawed spouses. We can either pretend we are not flawed and thus live divided lives, or we can live in the light, "as he is in the light" (1 John 1:7), and activate what we need in order to become good gifts to our spouses. Our former participation in an idolatrous culture—and the lure of that culture, although we have broken bonds with it—means that we may never attain a pristine ideal of chastity, even in the best of marriages.

We can, however, be held to *justice*. That means making every effort to give the beloved his or her due. That means we reveal ourselves in our marriages: all that we are and are not yet. It means to lay aside all investments in persons and habits that war against fidelity to the spouse. In the light of temptation, and the threat

---

[93] Pieper, *The Four Cardinal Virtues*, 79–80.

of moral failure, we tell truth to supportive chaste friends who strengthen our yes to the vows we've made. In the case of failure, we seek restitution. That means owning the failure, seeking the spouse's forgiveness for doing damage, and ascertaining what needs to be fortified to ensure sobriety and the rebuilding of trust in the marriage.

The way forward involves both freedom *from* and freedom *for*. We want to be free from disordered desires, but for what? Knowing the answer involves ascertaining what freedom means to both spouses regarding sexual expectation and pleasure. Annette and I have had seasons of heightened sexual activity and lean seasons. There is no right or wrong regarding the change of seasons; what matters is revealing one's desires and frustrations to the other.

Real chastity involves giving oneself to the other according to his or her expressed good. If my desires are compulsive and construed by Annette as using her, I withdraw. If she expresses longing and I am aloof, I need to consider that and seek to offer myself in a way that pleases her. If, for extended times, we cannot come together physically, then we are grateful for the seasoned graces we activate to steer clear of counterfeits. For me, this involves releasing every temptation to erotic images and masturbation; for Annette, it means avoiding media opportunities that fuel a kind of romantic lust. We seek freedom from such things in order to remain true to each other.

Our freedom to become one is a sacred trust—it is the one thing we share in our marriage that we will never share with another human being. This is justice—ascertaining and giving the other what is due to him or her. My body belongs to Annette and hers to me. We must, then, make every effort to keep this most distinctly marital aspect of our relationship alive and well. Such vitality insists that we speak of our sexual needs and assess them together at different stages of life. Just as St. Paul likens becoming one in marriage to Jesus' full revelation of Himself to His Bride, the Church, so do we in marriage reveal ourselves to each other. We walk in the light of His yes to our chastity, which only has meaning if we reveal our sexual needs and find the way to love our spouse well. The only way forward is in the light.

———

I have great hope for marriages shaken by the reemergence of old destructive patterns. There is a way forward for the formerly divided—and still vulnerable—to be just and true in marriage. Never easy, of course! It takes honest effort to reveal oneself. It also requires a common language and expectation of what to share, when, and how much. Securing a set time each week to check in on these loaded issues can be helpful. More than anything, it means trusting God in respect to this other whom we love but cannot control.

Our *pretty good* marriage was a solid base on which Annette and I have labored for over forty years helping persons—single and married—sort out a host of sexual problems. Annette specialized in accompanying Christian women whose husbands had not been faithful. These men had not adequately faced and addressed their moral weaknesses and failures prior to marriage. For the most part, they sought marriage as a way of curing their addictions. Inevitably, these unexpressed weaknesses became strongholds of wickedness in their marriage. The guilt of violating a spouse drove sins underground until they surfaced in painful ways. We can say assuredly: rather than curing sin, marriage exposes it.

Two areas that inevitably came to light in these marriages were same-sex attraction and pornography addiction. What might freedom from these two persistent sources of conflict look like for a marriage? How can justice be served when these forces are at play?

First, same-sex attraction. Because this longing arises from different sources, there is no one template that applies to all. What is probably common for most orthodox Christians is the shame that shrouds this longing for physical and emotional fusion with one's own gender. Shame shuts us up—the smog that hovers over past relationships with "gay" porn or friends silences the fact of these longings. One must reveal oneself: "Quite apart from what I want, I wrestle with these feelings." The truth: one is not intrinsically "gay," feelings come and go, and one typically neither asked for nor delights in this inclination.

Let your spouse or fiancé in! Believe me: any conflict in marital desire will be exacerbated by saying nothing. Do not try and work it out on your own. Cry out for mercy with the help of this person who loves you.

Had I not had Annette, who knows where I would be today? She did not personalize my temptations; she knew they preexisted the marriage. She extended the grace of marriage to me, which freed me from prowling outside the marriage for illicit love. My occasional experiences of same-sex attraction in no way voided my love for her. Bringing them into the light of spousal love intensified gratitude for her and freed me to offer myself to her with integrity.

Temptation did not tag me as a "gay" spouse. I hate that language. It's inaccurate. I am a man created for one woman. Period. Anything less than that is an affront to our entire family. My will and my energies are directed to her and to the well-being of our children. That is the definitive truth: the only *just* definition of a person with same-sex attraction who chooses to pursue marriage.

I say "just" because every spouse deserves to be loved undividedly. I chose Annette because I wanted her more than any other person. I, a man, said yes to one woman. And she, knowing my history, said yes to this man. We both closed doors to other lovers when we sealed our lifelong commitment to each other with our bodies. We declared then, as we do today, that we will not siphon those energies off elsewhere. We will submit our weaknesses, one to another, but we will not tolerate wickedness, including the definitions and practices of alien LGBT+ "selves." That is adulterous, divided, and unchaste.

Cultural shifts necessitate that people with same-sex attraction work out their motives, and their resolve, to love undividedly in marriage. Why? The world is now "out and proud"; we celebrate what used to be shameful and hidden. Persons who are still vulnerable to the lure of "gay" identification and lovers need to demonstrate the fruit of closing the door on those temptations. The seductive powers-that-be are much more persuasive now. The untested struggler who marries in the hope of bypassing that seduction needs to think again. So does the partner.

I say again to the struggler: Know yourself. Repent at the source—your inner desires and motives. Do so repeatedly until you have died to LGBT+ options. Make sure that door is closed before marriage, or in the case of a broken marriage, make sure that door gets closed for justice's sake—for the sake of what your spouse deserves. When our common enemy bangs on that door from without, learn to turn to the right sources to stay true. Reveal yourself and your struggle over and over until you are chaste—you will be weak at times, but you will not relent to the counterfeit.

The same counsel can be applied to all persons—male or female—who have a history of porn addiction. As most young males, and many young females, are exposed to porn repeatedly before marriage, couples should ascertain how habitual this sin has become. Again, marriage alone will not cure this addiction—one must demonstrate mastery over porn use prior to the wedding. Any addiction is fueled by stress and insecurity, and marriage is full of both. One must demonstrate an awareness of his or her addictive tendency and set controls in place to ensure justice in the marriage.

Offering one's sexual gift to naked persons on a screen is *idolatry*—false worship—and *adultery*—taking a lover other than your spouse. It is unjust and dangerous to all persons influenced by you, especially your spouse and your children.

My first exposure to porn was through a family member. His use of the poison stoked my own lust. The sins of family members can transfer to other members. I was admittedly greedy and devious in partaking of another's idolatrous "stash." But it was available in my house; other gods were worshipped there. That convicted me. When I became a parent, I developed a godly fear of my kids being predisposed to the sexual idolatries of my youth. The only way of assuaging this fear: keep my house free from the idolatry of porn. I made that choice, and keep making it, for my sake and for the sake of all who pass through my family. Repent and bring forth the fruit of repentance.

What does this mean? Reveal yourself. Make known historic porn use to spouse and trustworthy friends. Work out a weekly, even a daily, accountability system with a couple of friends. Put controls on your devices so you cannot readily access porn. Keep revealing yourself. It is okay to be known as someone who is vulnerable to smut. I feel as if porn bore spiritual holes into my eyes that keep me vulnerable. I'm okay with that. Live in the light of Jesus, His people, and your spouse. Serve justice to others, especially your spouse, with your sobriety. One day at a time.

Through sobriety, fathers set a precedent for their families. We serve justice in this virtual age, when male children will, on average, be exposed to hardcore porn on the Internet at thirteen years old.[94] Our living honestly and decisively in the light of our own vulnerabilities grants us authority; it frees us to equip our children to forego poison with equal candor and conviction.

I won't soon forget one hot summer night when my eleven-year-old came home wearing a thick coat in which he hid approximately ten porn DVDs acquired from a friend. He was embarrassed, of course, but it freed me to speak honestly about the hazards of porn: "It ignites you but reduces your freedom to love a whole woman. Instead of making you a good lover, porn breaks you and makes it tough to desire and to love a real, imperfect person. That's why St. Paul calls us in the power of the good Spirit to put to death the acts of the flesh (Gal 5:16–26). Porn is one such 'act' we can kill."

The next day we did just that—we started a bonfire, smashed the DVDs with an axe, and threw the pieces into the flames. My son felt empowered to kill porn before it killed a part of him. My own past, which my son knew enough about, gave me authority to show him mercy but also to serve justice—to equip him to do at that point in his life something I wish I had learned to do years before.

Another father, Jim, a friend of mine, was concerned and enraged over his teen son John's foray into homosexuality. Jim had found "gay" porn and evidence of a same-sex relationship on John's phone. That floored the orthodox, macho father. He hated homosexuality because, as a kid, he had been abused for years by an uncle. I urged him to treat his son mercifully, as a needy kid who especially needed his father's love now. That was tough for them

---

[94] *Fight the New Drug*, "What's the Average Age of a Child's First Exposure to Porn?" accessed January 28, 2020, *Fight the New Drug*. https://fightthenewdrug.org/real-average-age-of-first-exposure/.

both, as Jim historically had been barely present for John, and he had just blown up at his son, taking his phone and essentially putting him under house arrest.

Soon after, Jim attended a men's retreat at his church, where two men who had been "married" testified to how Jesus was calling them to Himself and apart from each other. They were winsome, humble, and grateful to God. Jim was undone. He had only experienced homosexuality as a grotesque threat, now embodied in his own son. Jesus invited Jim to see the problem through His healing gaze. The two formerly identified "gay" men shared their father wounds and how God the Father was healing them, in part due to the advocacy of their newfound church brothers. Jim broke down and opened his wounds of abuse to the mercy of the sensitive men there who prayed for him and helped him to forgive his abuser.

Jim repented that weekend of his irrational fear and hatred of homosexuality; he also owned the fact that his absence in John's life had contributed to his son's problem. He repented of neglect—turning to John in admission of the sin that he did not know his own son. Jim took responsibility and began to father John. His repentance served justice, activating the father to give the son his due through the gift of himself and his extra time. He continues to attend to his son deliberately, tenderly, and consistently.

———

What about spiritual fathers? I refer specifically to priests who take a vow of celibacy. How does real celibacy serve justice to a priest's spiritual children? How do broken vows violate justice for the faithful?

I rejoice in the many gifts I have experienced from good priests. Though I embrace my vocation as a father and husband, and I actively take my place in the Church in the priesthood of the baptized, I rely upon the structure and function of the Catholic priesthood, particularly to administer the sacraments. I realize that these sacraments are valid even if priests are in a state of moral disorder. Like you, I long and pray for their integrity. Yet I agree wholly with St. Augustine who, while parsing the Donatist heresy, made clear that the sacraments remain efficacious even when priests are full of sin.

Still, I am grateful and hopeful because of well-ordered, chaste priests from whom I have benefited. I can testify about them that my own confessions of sin and disorder have been met with words of wisdom and healing counsel. We need men who know themselves and Jesus well enough to accompany us into further integration.

As a father seeking to be undivided in my spiritual and bodily self, I need fathers who are one step ahead of me in that integrity. How else can I wholeheartedly serve justice to my children? A whole-enough priest, who has faced his passions and found a way forward to forgo marriage for the Kingdom's sake, is a gift that keeps on giving.

It is right and just that the man who has made a vow of celibacy is living that vow; a priest serves justice to the unchaste by continuing to grow in chastity. I have known several priests reasonably well and can attest to their authority to strengthen my yes to sobriety and order in my marriage. I know this authority is founded on hard work. That involves their own daily yes to chastity and the acquired solidity of striving to live a whole life, undivided by distractions of the flesh.

As a member of Christ, I deserve that integrity from persons who represent Him in the priesthood. That is my due. Priestly order helps me to be ordered — to emulate Jesus' wholeness and to prepare myself, my family, and others to be a whole Bride. Priests facilitate those goals by embodying the progressively holy state to which we all aspire. I know that fundamental integrity involves a long process of discernment and training in virtue. I trust that priests-in-the-making and priests, once ordained, will walk circumspectly with wise guides.

I deeply respect the work of a particular seminary—Kenrick-Glennon in St. Louis—that coined the term I have used often in this chapter—"Reveal yourself"—as the credo that informs the main value seminary leaders seek to instill in their charges. In other words, they urge young aspirants to become holy by being ruthlessly honest—decisive and candid about fleshly divides and ardent in loving people clearly, wholly, and chastely. Leaders at Kenrick-Glennon are not concerned about propping up weak persons in order to turn out large numbers of priests; they seek to prove men's integrity by how forthrightly they reveal weaknesses and how strong they have become in holy power. Kenrick-Glennon would rather dissuade unchaste men from pursuing the priesthood than prop up immature ones as "fathers" of the faith.[95]

In other words, Kenrick-Glennon seeks to discern and find men who seek to cover their emotional and sexual deficits in vestments. Arguably, this lack of discernment has been a source of much trouble—grotesque injustice—for Church members subject to priests who have used the collar to dodge the hard work of becoming men. A friend of mine said: "Because of my homosexuality, I knew I could not be a normal father. So I became a spiritual one."

We all know the story: a bright, devout boy who may well be inclined to a deep spirituality but who does not relate well to peers is fast-tracked to seminary. He hides his same-sex attraction

---

[95] Susanne Harvath, Paul Hoesing, Ed Hogan, and Jim Mason, *Seminary Formation and Transitory Same-Sex Attraction: A Proposal* (St. Louis: Kenrick-Glennon Seminary, 2019).

due to shame and guilt, is targeted by similarly inclined elders in seminary, and abused — confirmed as one of "them." Perverted fathers passing down their empty way of life.

Many Catholics don't think this through. I heard this from a Polish deacon, healthily married and orthodox, about an evidently "gay" priest and friend who was acting out sexually in a monastery: "But what else is he going to do?"

How about he gets help and not use the Church as a cover for his sin?

We cannot pretend that we do not have a "gay" problem throughout the worldwide Church. Though the United States has made strides in breaking up strongholds of "gay" culture in seminaries and diocesan life, it remains a problem. Outside of the more skeptical and secular west, many cultures champion the sanctity of priests, regardless of what they do in private. Protect the priest at all costs! My colleague Benjie, who grew up in the rural Philippines and is the Living Waters National Coordinator there, was raised by staunchly Catholic parents. His father farmed him out to the local priest, who was known to be a predator and who used eight-year-old Benjie to satisfy his lusts. Benjie's dad deemed the priest's "needs" more important than the dignity of his own son.

Two men with two very different axes to grind about the Church nevertheless came to the same conclusion: the Church has become a refuge for male leaders with same-sex attraction. One of them is far-left French LGBT+ journalist Frederic Martel, and the other is far-right Archbishop Carlo Maria Viganò.

Martel's *In the Closet of the Vatican* claims to unearth rampant hypocrisy in the Vatican, a tiny nation that he says supersedes San Francisco's Castro District as one of the biggest "gay" communities in the world (although his 80 percent estimate, which he claims is based on multiple sources, strikes me as inflated).[96] According to Martel, "gay"-inclined boys in Europe found in the masculine universe of seminary life and the priesthood an excellent escape route. This trend, Martel hopes, is ending as liberated Europe now frees young men to embrace their LGBT+ selves and forego the "myth" of chastity.[97]

Martel, a non-Catholic, loves all things LGBT+, so he "could care less if priests betray vows of chastity"; what he hates is the priestly hypocrisy of vowing one thing and doing another.[98] "Never have the appearances of an institution been so deceptive; equally deceptive are the pronouncements about celibacy and vows of chastity that conceal a completely different reality."[99]

Whatever you think of his politics, I think Martel rightly links a large percentage of men with same-sex attraction with those who cover up underage sexual abuse by priests. Martel recognizes adult same-sex desires as different from lust for children, but he sees the secrecy in the first area as contributing to silence in the second. "The culture of secrecy needed to maintain silence about the prevalence of homosexuality in the Church has allowed abuse to be hidden—for predators to act."[100]

This lines up with what we know about children who have been sexually abused by priests. The most comprehensive data—the John Jay College of Criminal Justice Report—reports that 81 percent of victims were male.[101] Boston's "Spotlight scandal" turned up

---

[96] Frederic Martel, *In the Closet of the Vatican: Power, Homosexuality, Hypocrisy* (London: Bloomsbury Continuum, 2019).

[97] Ibid., 8, 414.

[98] Ibid., 252.

[99] Ibid., x.

[100] Ibid., 92.

[101] The John Jay College of Criminal Justice, "Executive Summary," *The Nature and Scope of Sexual Abuse of Minors by Catholic Priests and Deacons in the United States 1950–2002*, (February 2004).

a similar figure: 85 percent of the fifteen thousand victims were males between the ages of eleven and seventeen.[102]

A recent comprehensive report by the Ruth Institute on the clerical sexual abuse scandal showed a growing "strong correlation between the percentage of self-described homosexuals in the Catholic priesthood and the incidence of sexual abuse of minors by the clergy."[103] Unlike the John Jay Report, or the Spotlight report, which dealt with cases reported from the sixties to the early eighties, the Ruth report includes current data.

We heard from Martel on the far left. On the far right, there is Archbishop Viganò. In the light of the sexual-abuse scandal with Cardinal Theodore McCarrick, Archbishop Viganò wrote a series of letters, beginning with his first bombshell on August 22, 2018.[104] Viganò claims the pontiff knew about McCarrick all along and simply turned a blind eye to his litany of homosexual seductions—both underage and adult. Whether Francis was truly complicit or not, Viganò brings to light what we can say now is true: the Roman Catholic Church is rife with same-sex-attracted leaders—some who undoubtedly walk in chastity, and others who, sadly, live divided lives, threaten to divide others, and bring disrepute on the name of Jesus.[105]

Viganò implores us: "We must have the courage to tear down the culture of secrecy and publicly confess the truths that we have kept hidden. We must tear down the conspiracy of silence with which bishops and priests have protected themselves at the expense of their faithful."[106]

---

[102] Ibid., 38.

[103] Paul Sullins, "Is Catholic clergy sex abuse related to homosexual priests?" (Lake Charles: The Ruth Institute, 2018).

[104] Carlo Maria Viganò, "Testimony," trans. Diane Montagna, August 22, 2018, https://online.wsj.com/media/Viganos-letter.pdf.

[105] Martel, *In the Closet of the Vatican*, 510

[106] Viganò, 1.

Whatever else he might be wrong about, Viganò is right about this. We've seen the same observation from both the far left and the far right. It cuts right across political divides. Silence is a sin against justice. It is unjust to the faithful.

———

I entered the Catholic Church in 2011, the year Pope Benedict XVI was perhaps most tormented by the hemorrhaging of the Church to homosexual abuse. Since then, I have watched how the abuse, and the scandals it caused, has damaged the most vulnerable of the faithful.

Priests who have dodged the hard work of growing up visit their immaturity on us all. I see this most clearly in bad counsel and shifty homilies in which boyish priests stammer about pressing issues as if they are unsure what the Church teaches. The Church is decidedly clear—it is the players who flinch and waver. This gap between priestly vows and virtue on the one hand and what is actually *lived* on the other creates a culture of hypocrisy that undercuts the Church's moral authority.

A divided priest also puts members at risk by developing unchaste relationships with either gender. Untrained in self-awareness and resistant to becoming known by brothers in his weakness, he misuses the power of his position. He treats others unjustly by making them emotional lovers. I have witnessed "special" friends of certain priests "helicopter" around them like mothers clucking after children. Sexual needs are expressed in real yet subtle ways; it can take months until the infatuation becomes physical. Then the narcissistic priest blames the sycophant, scapegoating the weaker one, who bears the shame and often loses faith as he or she staggers toward the wilderness.

Perhaps we err in citing childhood abuse as the main fallout from unchaste priests. Far more prevalent are the subtle but powerful abuses of disordered adult relationships orchestrated by the needy priest. These misuses of priestly power and office are altogether unjust.

Tolerating priestly abuses may well weaken the gospel that transforms lives. In my Catholic circles, I do not often witness the gospel applied powerfully for the setting free of sexual sinners. Where is evident, truthful, and compassionate help for them in our Roman Catholic Church? Our lack of clarity may well stem from powers-that-be who aren't sure there is life beyond sexual sin, and whose unbelief grows in a culture of secrecy.

Our shrouded hope is unjust. Our gospel may well be "veiled to those who are perishing" in sin (2 Cor. 4:3). Listening to Jesus' still small voice, an anonymous Benedictine monk heard this: "Until My bishops and My priests allow Me to wound them with the fiery arrows of My divine love, their own wounds—wounds of sin—will continue to fester and spread a filthy infection of corruption and impurity in the Church."[107]

Mercy is key. Repentance unto mercy is how we can restore robust chastity. That begins with each of us, priest and layperson alike. I have pointed out some of the injustices of sins against chastity upon marriage and church life. We must look at the cost of divided lives with our hearts and eyes wide open. Pieper rightly points out how "mercy without justice is the mother of dissolution": it would be too easy to try and swath our sexual mess in a big, merciful diaper—"judge not," etc.[108] That "mercy" alone, however, would not heal our wounds. We must face the wound with justice in order to value mercy and extend it properly.

[107] A Benedictine Monk. *In Sinu Jesu* (New York: Angelico Press, 2016), 161.
[108] Pieper, *The Four Cardinal Virtues*, 112.

Yet extend mercy we must—to ourselves, to our wounded friends, to our leaders, to all our unchaste "frenemies." "For justice without mercy is cruelty."[109] We are all victims and perpetrators of the fallout from an unchaste Church and world. No one of us is untouched—whether our divides originated from our sins or another's more obvious sins, we can heed Jesus' invitation to reenter the mercy pool, ever replenished from His wounded heart and side. I, for one, am reminded daily of how near I live to dissolution, and how only mercy—Jesus' continual call of love and divine friendship—is my cure and defense against reinfection. Perhaps no one is wholly free from the adultery of the heart engendered in all citizens of an idolatrous world.

As we are dragged before a group of law-abiding elders in our adultery, we can welcome Jesus (John 8:1-12). We are each that adulteress, rightly accused of a divided heart and scorned by our own internalized shame. After a while, you don't need a tribunal—you become your own best assassin. We need to allow Jesus to serve justice to us, His way.

First, Jesus refuses to dialogue with our accusers; He just bends down and considers how the law-abiding fail to deal with their own sins and so refuse the mercy that could be theirs.

Second, He commands: "Let any one of you who is without sin be the first to throw a stone at her" (John 8:7). Waiting guilty on the firing line, we hear only the sound of stones falling in the sand.

Having silenced our accusers, He then (thirdly) invites us out of condemnation and into chastity. We can leave our "life of sin" (John 8:11) because merciful Jesus goes before us and with us, making and enabling the way for our freedom.

[109] Ibid.

Mercy is not opposed to justice but rather expresses God's way of reaching out to the sinner by offering him a new chance.... God does not deny justice. He rather envelops it and surpasses it with an even greater event in which we experience love as the foundation of true justice.[110]

Love is the foundation of true justice for the unchaste person aspiring to wholeness. What are some keys to accessing this merciful love and to serving justice to others in our fragile stability?

First and foremost, we must brand ourselves with Kenrick-Glennon's credo: "Reveal yourself." For mercy to become our freedom, we must break the silence that has divided us and potentially demonized others. That is our responsibility—each one of us, regardless of vocation.

One must be wise about this, of course. Today's Church is a landmine of lawsuits, bankruptcies, and political fears of "being found out." One could say it is not a safe place to be known. This mistrust is strengthened by an already uncomfortable silence related to priestly celibacy; there is a kind of unspoken rule that priests should not share openly about how they manage their affections. I have found a difference here compared to the ease with which many Protestant pastors speak candidly about their efforts at purity.

That being the case, we must find a way! The Holy Spirit said pointedly to me early on in my marriage and ministry: "Don't ask me to set you free if you are not willing to be utterly honest about your sin." In other words, you enslave yourself to sin unless you "reveal yourself."

Both the vows married people make to each other and the vow a priest makes of celibacy call us to "reveal ourselves"—to take responsibility for others, to know ourselves honestly and consistently.

---

[110] Pope Francis, Apostolic Letter *Misericordiae Vultus* (April 11, 2015), no. 21.

How else can we give others their due if we have not secured safe places where we can aspire, one day at a time, to real chastity?

Obviously, in marriage, that means we make every effort to love our spouses with integrity and clarity, shoring up weak areas with solid accountability outside the marriage, to which the spouse should have ongoing awareness.

For priests, this is a greater challenge. Who knows him? To whom can he go regularly to work out conflicts of desire and habit? Marriage provides a relational spotlight—for better or worse—that reveals the dirt consistently. For the priest, finding partners that are near enough to become safe and powerful lights and points of connection can take time and a concerted effort. But it is an effort priests must make. The integrity of the Church depends on it. We, as members of Christ, need priests who embody the goodness of the celibate call.

How to do this? I like the metaphor of a mercy pool, because I think any honest progress in chastity must involve "soaking" in mercy for a while. We need to be aware of God's mercy. We need to understand that injustices must be repaired. We can come to know those truths and *integrate* them—make them part of who we are—only through repeated acts of community life. Sexual sins and wounds are inherently hidden and mask an authentic need for love and connection. The only way to meet that need is to connect in the light, over and over, with trustworthy walking partners.

Alcoholics Anonymous gives us a good template. In a manner not unlike AA, we who have compromised our callings need to learn how to gather, share, pray, and authentically father each other into freedom. I love this: not so much the standard model of "healthy" professional caring for a patient, but a band of brothers, admittedly broken, who learn to care for each other over the long haul. I have experienced different expressions of this (including

Living Waters), where men from various backgrounds gather to help each other grow in chastity. The more diverse, the better!

All it takes is a couple of relatively mature people with a vision and a willingness to make a way for others. All benefit from such a community; leaders do not exempt themselves from entering with their sin and need. For example, in the current Living Waters offering I help run, I lead a small group composed of a priest, a therapist, a school principal, and a couple of lay leaders. Every day, we share our efforts to overcome various addictions; we are also learning how to know and pray for each other in deeper areas of need. Awesome! We are known and loved together. We are experiencing a nearness of Jesus in our weaknesses and are growing in holy strength. That applies not only to overcoming sinful habits but also to loving others more responsibly in our lives. We are becoming more mature men. Together.

To be effective, such a group requires leaders who can establish solid boundaries and expectations, and navigate the demands of justice with mercy. It is all too easy to swathe a person in mercy. That's essential, but we must also maintain a bigger picture of this man's responsibility for others. For example, a husband overcoming porn (or another addiction) must be aware that his failures directly impact his wife. An addicted single person must be reminded constantly that the gift of his personhood needs to be given constructively to others.

Each man's affective maturity—his capacity to recognize the impact of his sins and how they rob others of what is due to them—needs to be considered in the group context. It is not just freedom *from* sin, it is always freedom *for* more mature expressions of one's gift. Like a good AA member, one can and should be reminded to make amends for the wrong one has done. We must live the truth that our actions impact those we love. We gather as sinners, not in a vacuum, but in order to mature in our real lives and to love others better.

I started this chapter with Roger and Kim's story of marital recovery. Roger, you remember, was narcissistic and had a series of affairs; Kim would need years of healing. They needed a small group surrounding them to help ensure justice for all, not just for Roger, charming sinner that he is. The most damaged person was his wife—and, indirectly, their children. Maintaining that view of justice, of what is owed to the ones our sin has damaged, is essential in responsibly inviting persons into the "mercy pool."

Finally, we must do everything in our power to ensure that the formation of young lives into the priesthood is grounded in reality—in the good, hard task of that man knowing and revealing himself. For too long, we have tolerated persons using the priesthood to avoid facing same-sex attraction, misogyny, various sexual and emotional sins, or any number of other blocks to natural fathering. Becoming a priest means renouncing a natural good—the gift of marriage. And that has to mean the would-be priest is whole enough to recognize that need and desire it.

Let's stop creating space in priestly formation for persons frustrated in their emergence as men. That is unjust and unmerciful. Like the remarkable Kenrick-Glennon Seminary, let us make every opportunity to forge real fathers from persons admittedly weak but authentically aspiring to holy strength.

Let us freely stop that process for those who buck at that integration. The people of God deserve holy, healthy fathers who promote good fathering for all. "A chastened priesthood will shine with chastity in the face of a world darkened by every fleshly vice and sinful excess."[111]

[111] A Benedictine Monk, *In Sinu Jesu*, 117.

This is not going to happen without hard work. And it's certainly not going to happen without honestly facing our sins and our brokenness. Whether celibate or married, we all have a mission to live in chastity, which means we're picking a fight with popular culture. And popular culture will fight back.

We need prudence to tell us what is real. We need justice to give others what is rightfully theirs. But to stick to those virtues in the face of constant opposition, we're going to need fortitude.

NINE

Fortitude and Integration

A musician friend of mine asked me to check out her videos on a catch-all website that was unfamiliar to me. To my chagrin, as soon as I pulled up her fine work, I was blasted by an array of porn ads. By God's grace, the porn ads had become toxic and unfamiliar to me, but they now smashed through the window of my heart like a rock thrown by an assailant.

It is humbling to describe how fast the old wound of corruption can be inflamed and how deep and dark the virtual sea invites our immersion. Before descending, I cried out for mercy and for my wife (which are related, thankfully) and averted a lost weekend. However, computer controls can't heal my old wound of corruption. Sensual idolatry beckons, and at times I long for that familiar plunge. I'm not proud of my residual temptations: still, they are inconvenient truths I declare to myself and my brothers daily in order to stay true to God and my wife.

Fortitude. Courage in the face of vulnerability. We've seen how prudence gives all the other virtues a foundation in reality, and how justice tells us how to balance what is right for ourselves with what is right for others. Now comes fortitude, without which we simply won't be able to exercise the other virtues.

Pieper rightly elevates our understanding of this third virtue by insisting that fortitude involves facing the "final injury," the threat of death or at least sizable diminishment of self. Fortitude demands a willingness to die, to surrender to something better, and to fight for it with all one has, regardless of the cost.

Honestly, I struggle to place my daily decision not to answer lust's beguiling invitation on par with martyrdom. Jesus frees me from lust for my good! I struggle with persons who whine about the loss of beloved idols when, in truth, idols want blood. Yet our saboteurs are persistent and can be as subtle as a touch, a glance, or some other human encounter that triggers a host of memories. Those of us weaned on the sensual gods must see reality clearly: we must rouse ourselves from the opiates that poisoned our dignity and happiness. For this, we must grow in fortitude.

Maybe this is a downsized version of moral bravery. However, it is essential to wholeness, for retrieving and reintegrating the parts of ourselves we gave away foolishly. Fortitude frees us for the long haul of becoming chaste.

We summon the courage to confess vulnerabilities. Fortitude frees us to tell the truth about what might otherwise consume us. Cowardice hushes us; we are silent because we are ashamed that we still struggle. Might it be that we have not seen reality clearly? If chastity has been misunderstood, then we may be under the presumption that we have become wholly chaste—we arrived, no longer pilgrims but now pious, even pompous citizens of a false heaven-on-earth. Fueling the farce may be the need of loved ones, especially one's spouse or close colleagues, to believe in our perfect integrity. Our prideful need to appear whole melds demonically with another's neurotic need for our perfection. Everyone fears relapse, so we create a static identity incapable of it.

In the spirit of St. John Paul II, we agree that Jesus frees us from the domination of lust. Although our disordered desire is decentralized (we give Him highest place now, not the worship of the creature), it may still rise in us and distort reality. We can still divide ourselves in duplicitous acts. In these times, wholeness seems ephemeral, as shifty as a cloud formation in a turbulent sky.

Here we summon fortitude. We tell the inconvenient truth of our conflict to ourselves and to our fellows. We hold fast to the truth of who we are and whose we are, beloved children of the Father who possess a more powerful spirit than the one animating our idols—the spirit of the Son Himself, through whom we cry out "Abba!" on the evil day (Gal. 4:4–7).

What, then, is going on here? Why does God allow His followers to be challenged so by waves of threatening desire?

———

Clearly, part of the fault lies in a world under the sway of forces that are unchecked in polluting our moral environment. Protective ozone layers are burned off, our bodies subject to hostile rays as never before. Pornography of every imaginable variety is available without limits to souls of every age, as are virtual communities that encourage lonely and vulnerable persons to take on an LGBT+ identity or worse. Seductive, even predatory bonds are forged long before the parent or pastor knows the conflict at hand.

We who aspire to chastity—especially those of us with same-sex attraction—are subject to ridicule. On one hand, we endure glamorous, sexy "takes" on LGBT+ possibilities in nearly every walk of life, polished up by media drivers. For those just getting a grip on chastity, this escalates temptation levels. At the very least, we are now hit by waves of new "converts" who, in everyday life, are utterly committed to boundary-violating intentions. What used to be hidden and shameful is now celebrated by "smart, compassionate" people who would be loath to disagree for fear of being framed as stupid or unloving.

We who resist for the sake of our integrity and for those we hold dear are now described as "haters" — seething with internalized homophobia — for daring to believe that something in us has fallen short of God's best for us. Encouraging others to aspire to more than mere longing for our gender is framed as dangerous, a threat to the fragile ecosystem of persons "born that way."

Methinks they protest too much. If LGBT+ identities are so substantial, then why do activists criminalize communities for thinking differently than they do?[112] We face great resistance — indeed, the diminishment of our integrity in the eyes of many — for daring to aspire to chastity. "We have become the scum of the earth, the garbage of the world — right up to this moment" (1 Cor. 4:13).

---

[112] The states of New Jersey, California, Oregon, Illinios, Vermont, New Mexico, Connecticut, Rhode Island, Nevada, Washington, Hawaii, Delaware, Maryland, New Hampshire, New York, Massachusetts, Colorado, Maine, Utah, and Virginia currently have statewide bans on "conversion therapy" for minors. Countries with nationwide bans include Brazil, Ecuador, and Malta. Canada, the United Kingdom, New Zealand, and Australia are considering bans. This list is growing and doesn't include states of the United States and countries that have bans on the city or provincial level.

Movement Advancement Project, "Equality Maps: Conversion Therapy Laws," March 20, 2020, https://www.lgbtmap.org/equality-maps/conversion_therapy.

Reuters, "Germany Moves to Ban Gay 'Conversion Therapies,'" March 20, 2020, https://www.openlynews.com/i/?id=48c05acf-118b-49a8-b82c-e93b50fa4ca3.

Fortitude. God calls us to live whole lives in the face of many divisive temptations. He exhorts us weak ones "to encourage one another daily ... so that none of you may be hardened by sin's deceitfulness" (Heb. 3:13). Could it be that He allows our heightened, prolonged battle for chastity to work in us a greater good, a more humble, tempered commitment to what is good and true and beautiful?

A light dawns and casts new meaning on the sheer depth and duration of the battle. What began as our desire to solve a messy "problem" has become in God's providence a converted life.

———

How does our battle become a conversion?

Thomas Merton writes of that little place of absolute poverty in us that is anointed to reflect the pure glory of God.[113] I relish this as I consider the residual weakness surrounding my sexual brokenness. God has trained me to know Him there, to discern its exposure (usually triggered by a seductive world), and to hide in the shelter of His wounds. I act by flinging myself upon His Crucified frame, which surrounds and astounds me with its power to secure me in holy love. Poverty, eclipsed by glory! For this, I rejoice in weakness. Through its depth and persistence, I have gained fortitude and have grown strong in mercy. How do I see this?

First, fortitude has taught me to choose the good in my moments of weakness. Only then can I know holy power. I do not mistake weakness for wickedness. When I submit disordered inclinations to demonic solutions, I become diseased by sin. No romancing "weakness" here; that is wickedness, and I go quickly to Jesus' members, starting with a priest, for my cure—the great exchange of sin for

---

[113] Thomas Merton, *Conjectures of a Guilty Bystander* (New York: Doubleday Religion, 1968), 158.

forgiveness. Fortitude has taught me something better: to endure temptation by opening up to mercy before the fall. I fall instead into Jesus, who is ever-ready to catch His weaker brother.

Secondly, I need fellow members to help me find this almighty, wounded God. We need to be known persistently in Christ's Body by friends who share our fight for chastity and who are willing to engage with us at the level of our vulnerability. They exist, and it is my duty to find them. In every parish I have joined, I trust that, in spite of compromised shepherds and sheep, God has set apart for Himself a handful of aspiring saints who have neither kissed nor bent the knee to Baal (1 Kings 19:18). Pieper's elegant proverb, "Because man by nature is vulnerable, he can be brave," means that I must bravely secure brothers if my vulnerability is to remain clean, free from the infection of sin.[114]

Some object to this type of community on the grounds that it will breed an ingrown subculture of sinners — "ex-gays," immoral rebels, disgruntled sinners who slyly encourage each other to accommodate sin on the grounds that the Church does not "get" us. Those of us who know what it means to worship Baal (or any fertility god or goddess worshipped through frenzied sexual expression) know better. No serious Christian should tolerate anyone who "misleads [Jesus'] servants into sexual immorality" (Rev. 2:20).

Fortitude insists that we become fierce in love toward each other, mercifully exhorting one another to more. Weak? You bet. And in our weakness, Jesus empowers us to discover together the narrow way that leads to life. Is this not the type of friendship that Pieper exhorts us to secure? He makes a strong case for prudent friendship: "It is possible for a friend — only for a friend and only for a prudent friend — to help with counsel and direction to shape a friend's decision or, somewhat in

---

[114] Pieper, *The Four Cardinal Virtues*, 117.

the manner of a judge, help to reshape it."[115] In a pinch, when worldly options beckon us away from His open wound, we draw wisdom and real courage from friends who strengthen and guide us. Fortitude frees us to bravely see and say that Jesus alone—secured by the communion of saints—surpasses all other gods.

I just met with a priest recently immersed in a Living Waters group who said this:

> For all my Christian life, I have been on the outside looking in at Jesus and Church, always feeling disqualified and failing to be chaste in a dozen small ways. Now I realize that I have never really welcomed Jesus and His mercy into my divided life. I have been trying to do it myself. I cannot anymore. At first, with these men, I could barely speak; I did not really grasp how you could be vulnerable yet brave, more united to the Love that is there than to shame and failure. Now I realize that Jesus wants to come into my divided life and help me, from the inside out. For the first time, I am known and helped by others who really know Jesus in this 'inside out' way.... I now know that I am deeply loved; I know He loves me, a weak man, His brother. I can tell you these things today, Andrew, because I am no longer a slave to fear, to judgment, the torment of striving on my own to be righteous. I am surrounded by others who, like me, are engulfed in mercy by His loving embrace.

Thirdly, I need the Eucharist to bravely endure little seductions for the joy set before me. Don't we all? Not one thing—no insight, no prayer, no gathering—can bring Jesus nearer, and bring Him

---

[115] Pieper, *The Four Cardinal Virtues*, 29.

more mightily, than the Host. He comes to us; He dwells in us, closer than a mother, a lover, or a brother. We can be brave at the core — right where we are most purely poor — because He endured His Cross in order to commune with us in His very essence. Poverty, swallowed up in glory!

I have known rich fellowship in a variety of ways — the Word dwelling among us through heavenly songs, preaching that searched out the deep things of God and human hearts, empowered prayers that shattered lies, and restored dignity. However, only the Eucharist anchors me wholly and consistently in Christ Crucified. I may or may not "feel" the Spirit resting on the meal. But I never fail to arise from that altar empowered by the brave one whose Cross-torn body, now crushed and consumed by me, makes me brave too.

I must underscore how "feelings" often belie what is actually occurring at the altar. Words nearly fail me here. I need the Host in order to be brave, to face what I must with the eyes of my heart fixed solely on Him. Maintaining that clear sight amid a host of seductive eyes is directly connected to Christ-in-me — the alliance of the "indwelt" heart and clean eye. Jesus said it best: "If your eyes are healthy, your whole body will be full of light" (Matt. 6:22). Holy Communion means just that — another dwells in us and clears the way for a chaste connection with others.

Perhaps, for that reason, I make every effort for daily Communion. I simply need Him in order to stay true to Him. Every day. Communion endows the weak with fortitude.

———

Pieper rightly points out how fortitude must conform to what is just and true. In other words, we must be brave for the right reasons. Jesus only blessed persons whose persecution resulted from righteousness, not foolishness. We risk and sacrifice for the good, for what conforms to reality. God made us for generous self-giving, to learn how to offer ourselves in ways that confirm another's gift while reinforcing one's own. That is the simple goal of our groups.

One such group in Paris, consisting of men and women aspiring to chastity, was infiltrated by a French reporter who, although a "gay" activist, pretended to submit his same-sex attraction for repair. He was treated openhandedly and with love; good efforts were made to help him receive the love of the Father through Jesus.

Little did anyone know that he was recording everything for a book intended to scandalize these humble aspirations toward chastity. He not only undermined the trust of persons seeking God and ordered relationships, he flat-out lied, distorting what occurred in the group into a gulag-like experience that, from his activist's viewpoint, was dangerous to the ever-fragile LGBT+ ego. In other words, he framed personal efforts to forgo "gay" identification as a violent assault on the "true" self. These French Christians have another idea on the true self: what that self can become through Jesus. My colleagues in France—merciful lay ministers—are being persecuted for what is right. The French media shames them relentlessly for their commitment to chastity and to serving persons who aspire to it.

They are brave for the sake of what is good and just. They carry their little crosses amid derision on all sides: from Christians divided by sexual sin who claim chastity is futile, and from a host of non-Christian activists who ascribe truth and justice to misbegotten identities.

Like St. Paul, my friends are struck down, but not destroyed (2 Cor. 4:9). In truth, the persecution they are facing—the shaking up of their everyday lives, the maligning of their names and vocations, the escalating threat of the state outlawing their good service—has become for them a badge of honor. "We are grateful to have a chance to carry our little crosses for Jesus' sake," said the senior leader.

They taste a bit of what Fr. Alfred Delp experienced in upholding human dignity under Hitler eighty years earlier. He wrote not long before his hanging:

> Perhaps what we modern people need most is to be genuinely shaken, so that where life is grounded, we would feel its stability; and where life is unstable and uncertain, immoral and unprincipled, we would know that, also, and endure it. Perhaps that is the ultimate answer to the question of why God has sent us into this time, why He permits the whirlwind to go over the earth, and why He holds us in such a state of chaos and in hopelessness and in darkness—and why there is no end in sight. It is because we have stood here on the earth with a totally false and inauthentic sense of security....
>
> Only where man does not cling inwardly to false security will his eyes be capable of seeing the Ultimate. Only then will he get down to basics and preserve himself and his life from these pedagogical terrors and horrors into which God the Lord must let the world sink, so that we—as St. Paul said—will awaken from sleep and see that it is just about time to turn around. It is just about time to change things....
>
> Where life rebels before your very eyes, you must set it right. These days, life lacks people who can come through the final shakings—with the knowledge and the consciousness: those who are watching for the Lord will not be affected, even if they are hunted off the face of the earth.[116]

[116] Alfred Delp, *Advent of the Heart: Seasonal Sermons and Prison Writings* (San Francisco: Ignatius Press, 2006), 41-43.

I am proud and empowered by persons who have come through serious shakings and have endured them in order to embolden those similarly shaken.

A good friend of mine, Anne, partnered with her husband in ministry to persons with same-sex attraction throughout the nineties. Both had early homosexual backgrounds, became disciples of Jesus, and found substantial help in various clinical and pastoral efforts. Under James Dobson's auspices, they received national attention with a *Newsweek* cover story that examined (somewhat skeptically) their claim to be happily married with three lively young boys.[117] Brave.

Based on that coverage, I chimed in on conversations with friends and neighbors and participated in Los Angeles-based media opportunities to herald how "coming out" wasn't the end of the line. Coming into Christ may well be the best and most wholesome move a "gay"-identified soul can make.

I ran into Anne and her husband several years later and was disturbed by his divided state. Post-ministry, his new business was infused with the LGBT+ set; he seemed to me to be relying upon old comforts and morphing into another "self." Not long after, Anne became aware of concrete ways he had violated his marriage vows, including identification as a "gay" man and eschewing any aspiration to a chaste marriage. Then, vilified by the LGBT+ community for having been an icon of everything they hated, he repented slavishly before them. He renounced as false any commitment to "change" and assumed full responsibility for damaging persons by his former aspiration to wholeness. Crazy.

Anne soldiered bravely on. She initiated a long process of separation, and ultimately divorced. As her marriage unraveled, Anne

---

[117] *Newsweek*, August 17, 1998.

began to partner with a few persons, including myself, to renew, equip, and unify a network of organizations that would fight for chastity on behalf of all persons impacted by the LGBT+ juggernaut. She led us well, and I grew to respect her greatly for her wisdom, humility, love, and most of all, her fortitude. In the initial stages of this new network,[118] she was still fighting for her marriage, hoping that her husband might renew his vows. Dismissing fears of infidelity until they could not be denied, she persevered in as humane a way as possible for all persons, especially her children, to quietly end the marriage. I stood with her during this formative period of the network and in her new phase of adapting to life as a single mother.

Anne exemplified the "patient endurance" that Pieper describes as the hallmark of fortitude. He claims that it is harder to endure than to be martyred. For orthodox Christians, the dissolution of a marriage due to infidelity is almost unbearable—a death to the most essential relational commitment one makes. It is a death one must endure patiently, especially when the unfaithful spouse claims his direction is prudent—conforming to the truth of things—and just, finally being "free" to live his "gay" narrative. Strange: we now ascribe "justice" to LGBT+-inspired infidelity and divorce on the grounds that the gender-bending, vow-breaking spouse just can't help it.

Anne refused to lose hope. In some ways, the dissolution of the marriage highlighted the fact of her courage and provoked it—the very reason she was standing stronger than ever for chastity. She lived the truth of what could be lost when a loved one refuses Jesus' way. She woke up every day to that loss and arose to uphold the hope of chastity to all who seek it.

---

[118] The Restored Hope Network, https://www.restoredhopenetwork.org/.

She realized the good by facing injury with courage—what is dreadful in order to realize the good.[119] She has continued to build, patiently and with integrity, a network designed to strengthen all who refuse to bend the knee to LBGT+ altars. She embodies "endurance, not wrathful attack, as the ultimately decisive test of actual fortitude—nothing else than to love the good and realize that which is good, in the face of injury and death, undeterred by any spirit of compromise."[120]

———

Fortitude must line up with what is just and true. It must actively be in service to actualizing what is good in the face of much resistance and opposition that may threaten one at one's core. Anne typifies this—as does my friend Sue, a devout Catholic mother who has endured the "coming out" of loved ones in her extended family. It seems to me that somehow women, in their profound connectedness to others, are perhaps more vulnerable than men to the impact of family members' poor moral choices.

Sue was born into a large family, where she, as the eldest, benignly accepted her Catholicism while learning how to care for her many younger siblings. She followed a traditional path of faith based on culture more than dynamic devotion; she married and raised her kids accordingly. All seemed fine until her young adult son "came out of the closet" and Sue had to discover, for the first time, what she believed about Jesus and chastity and redemption. Another loved one "came out" and later claimed to be exploring "transitioning" to the other gender.

Around this time, I, as a young Catholic, was seeking anyone via the parish bulletin who wanted to pray with me about our Church

[119] Pieper, *The Four Cardinal Virtues*, 127.
[120] Ibid., 131.

mess: the shame, hurt, mistrust, and hope for the healing our parish sought after a pedophile priest had ravaged the flock a year before.

Sue would not have defined herself as unchaste. But she knew something about sexual brokenness. She was just waking up. By her own admission, she had lived a dull and disengaged Catholic life. She now wanted to know Jesus—for herself and for her loved ones.

Most of her extended family celebrated the LGBT+ reality and thought she was nuts for thinking otherwise. Sue wanted to know what Jesus thought. For the first time, she was experiencing what it meant to stand bravely with the merciful Jesus and what He asks of His disciples. Sue had discovered her little cross amid this suffering. And she vowed to love well through this fire, as it burned off mere conformity to a "culture" and invited her into the cruciform life.

We partnered. We prayed. I invited Sue to join a host of strugglers aspiring to chastity who "grasped and clung vigorously to what was good."[121]

Sue's commitment to becoming authentically moral was harder. It divided her family, whose members meant more to her than anyone else. Though she couldn't relate to some aspects of sexual disintegration, she learned to read her own divides: people-pleasing, denying the truth in the face of family and friends to save face. She discovered something about making the family an idol. In a way, she had failed to worship the Creator and had bowed before an image of family harmony. She learned, painfully and daily, what the *Catechism* means when it says that "family ties are important but not absolute"[122] She began to learn the harder way of love founded on Jesus, the Absolute. She became a mother who put her faith first: a stench to some, a fragrance to others (2 Cor. 2:16).

---

[121] Ibid., 128.
[122] *Catechism of the Catholic Church*, 2232.

What Sue embodied, and what we learned most from her, was how to love persons who not only do not love Catholic reality but whose choices fly in the face of that reality. Sue loved. Her fortitude exemplifies this vigorous clinging to the good, not denying its inconvenient truth, but bearing with loved ones who refuse the truth. I love how Sue does this! She makes sincere efforts to serve loved ones who oppose what she holds most precious. Truly, this is patient endurance: bearing with our precious ones confused by untruth, hoping that divine love will prevail in the end. *When* and *how* remain questions along Sue's little way of love. More than once, we grieved with her as she shook with sorrow over the destructive impact of this untruth.

She had much to shake off—much that needed to be burned up in the fire of holy suffering. She had to let go of expectations of "normal" family life, let go of grief over her own little losses, let go of envy over friends whose loved ones exemplify the virtues as they multiply members, let go of and guilt—guilt-upon-guilt for somehow contributing to a loved one's identity confusion. We who came from broken backgrounds helped Sue a lot here. We helped her see the difference between inclination (many factors, including parental influence) and adult identity formation, for which each person must take responsibility. No one but the individual assumes an LGBT+ persona. We strengthened Sue to welcome forgiveness where she perceived failure and to give each person the dignity to choose how to resolve "inclination." We stand alone before Jesus in this choice.

We may have helped Sue to endure, but she *exemplified* endurance. Her fortitude made us brave as she bore her unique cross. Dietrich Bonhoeffer, the German theologian who bravely faced his own execution by the Nazis, describes this mark of fortitude beautifully:

> Perseverance, translated literally, means remaining underneath, not throwing off the load, but bearing it. We know much

too little in the church today about the peculiar blessing of bearing. Bearing, not shaking off; bearing, but not collapsing either; bearing as Christ bore the Cross, remaining underneath, and there beneath it—to find Christ.... Remaining steadfast, remaining strong is meant here too; not weak, acquiescence or surrender, not masochism, but growing stronger under the load, as under God's grace, imperturbably preserving the peace of God. God's peace is found with those who persevere.[123]

Something extraordinary came out of Sue discovering Jesus under this cross. She became a life source to others. Like Anne, Sue gathered other parents and family members of LGBT+ loved ones to help them bear their burdens well. And she discovered many spiritual sons and daughters who wanted to walk the way of chastity yet needed support and encouragement. As Sue persevered with her own extended family, she discerned that God was expanding her notion of family. God multiplied her maternal gift: members of Christ whose lives got rocked by the LGBT+ juggernaut rediscovered their hope in Christ, in part through Sue's witness. Her maternal love was an answer to Jesus' question: "Who is my mother, and who are my brothers? Here are my mother and my brothers.... For whoever does the will of my Father in heaven is my brother and sister and mother" (Matt. 12:48-50). Sue is among them, beloved of her Father and surrounded by His children.

Patient perseverance, clinging to the good without compromise, enduring diminishment of self for the greater good: these are the hallmarks of fortitude I have witnessed in my friends. Fire for chastity burns a hole in the door slammed on them by the world

---

[123] Dietrich Bonhoeffer, *A Year with Dietrich Bonhoeffer: Daily Meditations from His Letters, Writings and Sermons* (San Francisco: Harper, 2005), 72.

and worldly church. Anne, Sue, and our Living Waters colleagues in France are steady flames of chastity, torches of divine love.

———

A key to their fortitude is a willingness to work hard to stay free for the fight. That means learning how to suffer well. Thomas Merton recognizes the temptation lurking in the most legitimate of sufferings. He writes: "Nothing so easily becomes unholy as suffering ... we can deny ourselves rigorously for the wrong reason and end up pleasing ourselves mightily with our self-denial.... To believe in suffering is pride but to suffer, believing in God, is humility."[124]

Fortitude is forged in the flames of divine love. Anyone who wants to know Christ must accept His invitation to share in the fellowship of His suffering (Phil. 3:10). What redeems suffering from self-congratulation is Jesus, who is ever present to draw us deeper into the sanctuary of His open side. There, united with His wounded Heart, we see not ourselves but the One who is making us new in our diminished state.

One committed to cross-bearing must be trained in this kind of union. Forging fortitude means learning to hide in the Sacred Heart of Jesus. No other way; no other place. In the most confusing, dismal moments, I dare not go elsewhere. Citing St. Thomas Aquinas, Pieper describes "the truly penetrating knowledge of things associated with an abysmal sadness ... which cannot be lifted by any natural force of knowledge or will."[125] Here deep calls to deep: Jesus is found not in a barrage of well-meaning words from creatures but in the main artery of His compassion—His wounded Heart, from which flows every sustaining mercy. Suspended like an infant in His wound, one can rest amid the battle, grateful for His impenetrable

[124] Thomas Merton, *No Man is an Island* (Bardstown: The Abbey of Our Lady of Gethsemani, 1955), 43–44.
[125] Pieper, *The Four Cardinal Virtues*, 121.

refuge. No room for religious preening here; glory lies in utter dependence. Christ is all. "Alleluia, all my gashes cry!"[126]

Yet even the humblest warrior can be derailed by despair. Enduring multiple losses for the Kingdom's sake takes a toll. For persecuted believers, a temptation lurks, not merely not to make one's bed but not to get out of bed at all! Here self-pity, discouragement, and unrelenting disappointment can converge into the "worldly sorrow [that] brings death" (2 Cor. 7:10). Pieper warns that such despair, however understandable, is "a decision against Christ . . . the most dangerous sin of all."[127] Why? Because despair casts us into a hell on earth. It refuses the light of life shining on the Cross. The one under the spirit of despair becomes blind to the good that only Christ can summon out of suffering.

Fortitude insists that we recognize this temptation and reject it, clinging to the good in faith. To forge fortitude, we wait for consolation, even as we continue the fight. We agree with the good. Always. In this way, God protects us from being made "inordinately sorrowful over evil and its injurious effects."[128] Here we are helped by wise, attuned members of Christ who may well discern our losing sight of His Cross in our obsession with our smaller crosses. Annette once saw me collapsing into darkness after myriad defeats converging on us from defectors and social-policy devolutions. I was ready to lay down my cross when she said, with inspired vitality: "Andy, wake up; this is where and why we need to stay true to Jesus and the battle for chastity!" Together, we surrendered afresh to His Cross and found refuge, a place to regain hope.

That does not minimize real losses. It simply means that in facing our losses, "we do not want you to . . . grieve like the rest

---

[126] Don W. King, C. S. Lewis, Poet (Kent: The Kent State University Press, 2001), 227.

[127] Josef Pieper, On Hope (San Francisco: Ignatius Press, 1986), 50-52.

[128] Pieper, The Four Cardinal Virtues, 129.

of mankind, who have no hope" (1 Thess. 4:13). Hope makes our grief good. Here the Holy Spirit empowers bravery. He is our ever-present advocate in hardships, in the forging of fortitude. God helps us to stay true to Him. The Holy Spirit is our abiding witness of the One who intends victory for us, come what may. The Spirit of the living God helps us stay tuned to God—our big victory—amid a hundred little losses.

The Spirit helps us in our weaknesses. I led a Living Waters training in Southeast Asia, where persons from a dozen nations gathered to grow in chastity and to equip others to do the same. Multiple assaults hammered us: conflicts intensified within our ranks and outside of us as reports of especially disturbing clerical abuse made headlines. Team members fell ill, and the needs of participants were overwhelming. After an especially difficult interchange with a close colleague, I believed there was no way to continue with the training.

I prayed with tears. The Spirit showed me a pool; I jumped into the clearest, soothing body of water imaginable, which had no end. It was a bottomless well that engulfed me and invited me to let go and just enjoy being suspended in God's most tender mercies. A host of troubles was no match for divine love; I was most aware that His depths were unfathomable, eternal. No matter how weighty the burden, the water was more buoyant still and boundless in its capacity to bear me up. I knew in an instant: divine mercy would suffice for us all. God would sustain our efforts and not forsake a single member of this training.

Through a minor vision, the Holy Spirit strengthened me to be brave. I could be brave because God, in His infinite mercy, made the way. "To be brave," says Pieper, "means not only to suffer injury and death for the realization of the good, but also to hope for victory."[129]

[129] Ibid., 141.

I came out of those waters upheld by hope and felt hopeful, ready to aspire for more. How could I not? At Calvary, Jesus poured out mercy without end; through Baptism, I came to life in His dying flood. The Spirit reminds me of this constantly, as He did for me in Southeast Asia, where He caused us to triumph. And He helps us today in our weakness. Whenever I lose heart in the fight for chastity, His spirit elevates my heart and helps direct it to the One who is our Source of all hope. He raises us from the down-drag of discouragement that can descend to despair. Hope wells up naturally from the Spirit, who groans deeper in us than any grousing about giving up. God our hope infuses us with hope, replenishing our fortitude in the fight for chastity.

That hope needs to be replenished constantly. The other day, harassed by internal ministry squabbles and a fresh round of LGBT+ accusations (how "toxic" our chaste aspirations!), and witnessing these pressures upon my wife, I felt wiped out, down for the count. I went to Mass and fell face down at the altar, certain that my rising depended wholly upon Another's. I just had to position myself before Him. Jesus likes my challenge. After all, did He not say: "Very truly I tell you, unless you eat the flesh of the Son of Man and drink his blood, you have no life in you" (John 6:53)? The Life we need to stay true, to renew our hope, to be restored after the tearing down—all contained in the Eucharist. The spirit of fortitude leads us to the table where we in our weakness are fortified for the fight. I left composed, clear-hearted, and strengthened.

I was ready to face all those pressures with a balanced and measured response. *Prudence, justice,* and *fortitude* had made me ready for *temperance.*

TEN

Temperance and Integration

I've witnessed the fruit of temperance in my friend Mike. He had been a house "divided against itself" (see Mark 3:25) by a host of adulterous behaviors. But he has worked hard to bring order into his own courts, and into his marriage.

His wife, Diane, suffered much from his divided life; she now reaps the benefit of his united life, lit from within and sustained by God's mercy.

Mike and Diane are the eldest children and most devout of two large Catholic families. Their difficulties—worked out after years in a closed community but opened modestly to others for their sake and in thanksgiving to God—have made them better. Their less faithful family members marvel and are convicted by their candid, cruciform marriage.

I will never forget the sight of the couple at Diane's mother's funeral. As we left the parish after Mass and slowly marched several hundred yards to the gravesite, Mike and Diane led the pack with a beautiful dignity. The chill of morning and loss was offset by this strong man who had been broken by intemperance and now lives an ordered life, for Diane's good. She was weepy and composed next to him. Something gorgeous flashed before me, a window of the divine. We followed the light of this couple whose life together invited us into saving grace, something of the Bridegroom gathering friends of the Bride. Marvelous, mysterious: the beauty of ordered life quietly consoling those who mourn.

Pieper says it best:

Not only is temperance beautiful in itself, it also renders men beautiful. Beauty however must be understood in its original meaning; as the glow of the true and the good irradiating from every ordered state of being, and not in the patent significance of immediate sensual appeal.[130]

Ten years later, Annette and I visited the two of them in the aftermath of Diane's first blast of chemotherapy for breast cancer. In the past, I have witnessed Mike angry and depressed, stuck in self and unwilling to meet Diane in her suffering, especially her pain related to his failures. But this was different. Mike rallied all his strength to make her as secure and comfortable as possible in this new fight. Though weakened by the battle, her head wrapped in scarf to hide her hair loss, Diane leaned back into this man, the two now contoured into a united front. Sex had nothing to do with it. Mike, now well trained in ordering his passions for the sake of another, exhibited a masculinity deeper than erotic need or appeal.

---

[130] Josef Pieper, *The Four Cardinal Virtues* (San Diego: Harcourt, Brace, and World, 1965), 167.

Pieper again:

The beauty of temperance has a more spiritual, more austere, more virile aspect. It is of the essence of this beauty that it does not conflict with true virility but rather has an affinity to it. Temperance, as the wellspring and premise of fortitude, is the virtue of mature manliness.[131]

Love tempered over time stands the test of time; it lights up the dark and reveals something of what virtuous humanity can be for one another. I relish this quote from Karol Wojtyla, who later became Pope John Paul II:

It is put to the test most severely when the sensual and emotional reactions themselves grow weaker.... Nothing then remains except the value of a person, and the inner truth of love comes to light. If their love is a true gift of the self ... it will not only survive but grow stronger, and sink deeper roots.[132]

Training in temperance, born of brokenness before God and primed by almighty mercy, has made Mike beautiful. It has given Diane the gift of exchanging anxiety for peace, a trustful composure that enhances her womanhood, even in distress. Wow. I am invited into something better, summoned to become a more temperate gift to Annette through their witness. I want to contribute to Annette's wholeness through my increasingly ordered life. I want something to flare up and warm her from my progressively ordered state!

[131] Ibid., 167.
[132] Karol Wojtyla, *Love and Responsibility* (San Francisco: Ignatius Press, 1993), 134.

Chastity cannot be understood without first grasping temperance: the ordering of the passions, including but not limited to sexual desire. What is this ordering? It involves integrating the various parts of oneself so that each "piece" is in proportion to the other. Pieper cites St. Paul's description in 1 Corinthians 12 of how Jesus creates a whole body by placing each member in the right proportion to each other.[133] Using the human body and its various "members"—ears, eyes, feet, etc.—as a metaphor for how each person in Christ's Body can and should exercise his gift in deference and gratitude to the other's, Pieper shows us a vision of how temperance helps order us as individuals.

Pieper gives us this macro vision from Scripture—the Body of Christ, one big temple composed of many parts, aspiring to its Head in cooperation with one another. Then he gives us its micro version, ordering our personal "temple" through the virtue of temperance.

Something is at work in us to dispose the various facets of our individual being into a unified, ordered whole.[134] Pieper is quick to point out how temperance is unique among the other four cardinal virtues in that it is concerned "exclusively to the active man himself"; temperance is the most self-concerned of the virtues, implying that "man should look to himself and his condition, that his vision and will should be focused on himself."[135]

———

Of course, ordering our various parts does not occur in a vacuum. The members of our personal humanity are created by God, and however disintegrated, something redemptive—the searching spirit

[133] Pieper, The Four Cardinal Virtues, 203.
[134] Ibid., 175.
[135] Ibid., 204.

of the Father and the Son who invites us continually into greater wholeness—is at work, summoning our fractured parts to cooperate with each other. The spirit of temperance is the Holy Spirit, who never ceases to invite us to give "greater honor to the parts that lacked it" (1 Cor. 12:24).

Might we consider that the spirit of temperance is also the spirit of divine mercy? How badly we divided ones need to know this God who woos us out of shameful and divided expressions of ourselves! He shines a light on the war within—our various parts and passions not in sync with each other but in conflict, sniping at each other, unable to help each other find their rightful place.

Let me give you an example from the premarital preparation Annette and I went through. The pastor accompanying us was also a psychologist who administered a rather intensive test to assess our mental health and the ways our profiles complemented or clashed with each other. No red flags, except for one: the test showed me nearly paranoid in my irrational belief that there were persons at any given time that opposed me and were rallying against me!

As we explored this further, I discovered that part of my disintegration as a man involved an overly emotional, subjective sensibility. I was passionate, yes, but my passion was not balanced with *reason*—a filter that could screen out my tendency to impose past hurts onto present situations. I had been bullied from midchildhood through my teen years because of my evident effeminacy. On several painful occasions, peers rallied to ridicule and accuse me of perversion. Since that time, having progressively shed my feminine affect, I still perceived male peers as suspicious and disdainful of me. In short, I was still way too subjective, guilty of framing innocent ones as perpetrators.

The pastor helped me to objectify. He summoned the good of reason—a "member" I possessed that could intervene in those moments where my faulty intuition suspected rejection. I learned to stop myself and dialogue with my skewed response. Blessed reason began to straighten me out.

That helped my relationship with Annette, as I was vulnerable to holding her to unfounded offenses. Temperance refined my touchy subjectivity; it helped to shore up the "weaker" part, thereby restoring "greater honor" to the deficient part (1 Cor. 12:24). Temperance helped prepare me for marriage by rounding out my gift of self for Annette.

The ordering of our personal temples is what temperance is all about. But as the last example clarifies, temperance has huge implications for interpersonal self-giving—how well we offer our personal temple to others. Pieper speaks of "selfless self-preservation," meaning that the goal of temperance is never just a gleaming saint rendered self-reliant by his "ordered" vessel but rather a person who is better able to passionately offer himself to others.[136] I love that.

Temperance does not diminish passion: instead, temperance connects our inner parts and reconciles us to "estranged" members. The result? Our passions are liberated to flow creatively, even exuberantly, for the good of others. Aligned with and activated by tempered desire, we reveal something about how we manifest God's image, His order. He made us and redeems us to become radiant expressions of Him. We can see how temperance—like the other three cardinal virtues—"enable man to attain to the furthest potential of his nature"[137]

In a moment, we'll get to how temperance helps channel sexual passion. But first, I'd like to highlight its value in directing anger constructively. We limit temperance by associating it mostly, even only, with sex.

[136] Ibid., 154.
[137] Ibid., 158.

Our passions cannot be limited to the sensual. Yes, conceiving life is essential, but we must also fight for life, fight for the good by summoning and directing passion to do so. Pieper writes: "At the mention of anger, Christian awareness sees as a rule only the uncontrolled, the anti-spiritual, the negative aspect. But as with 'sensuality' and 'desire,' the power of wrath also belongs to the primitive forces of human nature.... Wrath is the strength to attack the repugnant; the power of anger is actually the power of resistance in the soul."[138]

Without reconciliation to wrath, we may well fail to aspire to something greater for family and culture. Pieper serves us well by describing true gentleness as a "virtue that presupposes the power of wrath; gentleness implies mastery of this power, not its weakening. We should not mistake the pale-faced harmlessness which pretends to be gentleness—often successfully—for a Christian virtue.... Such incapacity is not a virtue, but as St. Thomas expressly says, a fault."[139]

I'll give you two brief examples of how temperance helped reconcile me to the good of my anger, thereby rescuing a rather smug gentleness from slumping into passivity and sloth.

After moving my growing family ten times in a decade throughout a grossly inflated Los Angeles, I was done. Gone was the "pale-faced" resignation to pouring money into crummy rentals and exhorting Annette to embrace our call as poor pilgrims who would never have a place all our own in a big city.

Then I got mad. She deserved better. My kids deserved better. I cried out to God and implored His help. He seemed to say He would help if I would do my part: His divine power would give me everything I needed for life and for godliness (2 Pet. 1:3). We had

---

[138] Ibid., 161.
[139] Ibid., 200.

little money, limited credit, and graduate school debt. With dim prospects, I was heartened by a call from a friend who was selling his house in a nearby small city that had just declared bankruptcy due to fiscal mismanagement.

An aberrant ebb of land value! A lawyer friend urged me to gather as much money as I could and act fast before the tide rose. I did, garnering the smallest down payment on record and banging on many doors, including forty banks that turned us down. The forty-first didn't, and I landed a home for us. Temperance insisted that anger pick a fight with passivity. Anger channeled into "selfless self-preservation," or at least a better life for my family, prevailed. Hail, holy spirit of temperance!

The second expression of wrath: in my new town of Kansas City, I caught wind of a bill that LGBT+ activists were pushing through the city council to ban therapeutic "change" efforts for minors with gender-identity problems. I could see right through it: kids with same-sex attraction or gender dysphoria would be barred from objective counsel as they sorted out questions about options related to gender identity conflicts. It was a big deal to vulnerable kids. A big deal to parents. A big deal for the One who designed them and has the power to redeem them.

Frankly, I was beat. We, as a ministry, were in an extended fast for friends and family of LGBT+-identified children, and the last thing I wanted to do was fight city hall.

But God stirred up my wrath. How dare these activists weave together a net of lies and cast it over the beleaguered, ignorant city council!

As we engaged with any city councilor who would talk, it became clear that they would listen to no other side but the "poor" victims charging deranged caregivers with multiple abuses that could not be corroborated.

The council was unfamiliar with the issues at hand and happy to go to bed with the pan-sexual, cross-dressing, lamenting lobbyists. When I had the chance to address the city council in its chambers, though I was flanked by a row of raging rainbow followers, I realized that any person seeking chastity was in truth the endangered minority in the room. The LGBT+ crowd was evidently carrying the day, and anyone seeking help, or helping a person resolve gender problems in a reasonable way, was framed as a nitwit. I cried out: "You are oppressing the most vulnerable—Christians who deserve the right to choose clinical care that aligns with their consciences!" With that, the rainbow wall exploded, the council looked down nervously, and soon after, the council members voted to pass the ban.

However, our tempered wrath caught TV cameras and the attention of a legal agency that is working hard to overturn what is clearly a violation of constitutional rights. Temperance invites wrath to burn up our "tolerance" of questionable precedents and gives us the moxie to fight for life—in this case, the rights of young persons to become their best: creative, ordered, and reconciled to the good of their gendered bodies. Selfless self-preservation: we fight for generations to come, for our children—the fruit of our own tempered love. That requires a wise assault on what masks as justice but is in fact repugnant. Temperance channels anger into fierce, focused resistance to injustice.

———

Pieper cites three factors that qualify temperance, all related to prudence. Temperance must correspond with the truth of how things are.[140] We must first be ordered to who God is, then secondly,

---

[140] Ibid., 173.

to who we are, made in His image, and then lastly, we must be ordered to the world—relating to others properly in a manner that corresponds to who they are.

Let's break this down a little bit. Let me draw on my own history of same-sex attraction, and how temperance helped order my humanity in this three-fold way.

1. First, *ordered to God*. We can be ordered to God only through humility—the progressive realization that He alone is God. We may well be aware—painfully and sensationally—of a host of desires coursing through us and conflicting us, like a convergence of turbulent streams that foment into one wild river. Yet self-awareness isn't enough. Only our merciful Father, summoned through Jesus, can compose us long enough to consider the best expression and direction of our passions.

Aquinas defines temperance as "serenity of spirit," as if this virtue invites us to look up and out from ourselves long enough to invite the source of serenity into our overstimulated frames. It makes sense to engage with the Creator as to how best to sort out our passions. He made us in His image, not the other way around; ordering our desires can and must involve the spirit of self-control that woos and persuades us to surrender to the source of our power of life and love. Then we can heed His still, small voice that speaks to us amid the turbulence.

I recall a riptide of same-sex desire that threatened to engulf me while I was a student at UCLA. There was much "gay" activity around me, which reminded me of my loneliness and my wearisome, eroding efforts to abstain. The waters were surging and threatening to break the embankments. Just then, I recalled the exhortation of St. Paul: "Walk by the Spirit, and you will not gratify the desires of the flesh" (Gal. 5:16). I pictured (with the eyes of my heart) opening my "river" to the One who made and loved me. I asked Him to ease the surging waters, to hold the banks intact, and to assume any pollutants I had poured in (old fantasies, memories). I praised Him right there: "Jesus, You know me, and You love me, a conflicted man. Thank You for upholding me—a sexual being—with a future and a hope. I don't know how You are going to help direct these desires unto life-giving purposes. But You are God, and I am not. You can do this. Jesus, I trust in You."

Temperance insists that we be ordered to the One who made us and who is intent on redeeming us. Right in the middle of our turbulence! The river flowing from His wounded side is ours for the taking: His flood of Blood and water pours into our stream of passion that seeks even in distress to achieve connection beyond ourselves. God is the first and most important source to whom we can open. That convergence of His Passion with ours sustains all progress in temperate desire.

2. But more needs to be done, which leads to the second point: being reconciled to how and who one is. I needed to make peace with the truth that—in spite of many desires—I was a man who needed to be reconciled to my own masculine essence. Common temptations involved abdicating my gender value to men I perceived as superior to me: bigger, stronger, more "realized" as men. My river wanted to jump its banks and somehow merge with one of them in a vain effort to become one with his essence, to be engulfed by it. That was a yearning for integration, for wholeness, yet in a disordered, self-deceiving way.

Sex only fractured me further by stifling real growth in masculine empowerment. The homosexual act torpedoes one's integration; it divides one further by firing up desire that intensifies with each new quest and exaggerates the expectation that another male becomes what he can never be. Why? It is contrary to the nature of things: to how God ordered us as men, and how we must be ordered to get on with the business of becoming men.

Temperance helped me get on track with the harder and more rewarding quest of making peace with the man I was. That occurred with the pretty good guys around me. These were Christian brothers who were intent on mirroring to each other something of the Father's love we shared as His sons.

3. On that basis, I could get on with the third dimension of temperance: ordering who I was to the world, to others around me, in a manner best for me and my brothers. I cannot underscore how crucial growth in temperance was to this task. My being—emotionally, physically, spiritually—needed to be ordered in such a way as to render me a good gift to others. While under the disordered notion that I and another man existed to "complete" each other, I would confuse and be a stumbling block to any community. What could be less prudent and more intemperate than imposing on a group my "gay" self? Unreality: assuming a "self" that knows no more becoming.

Still, I had to walk with my heart's eye wide open, my little cross steady before me. Why? I had a great fear of messing up—of falling back into old unrealities—*en route* to becoming a temperate friend to others. On several occasions, I experienced some attraction for friends whose trustworthy love tempted me to make them something that they never could be. Facing that fact, eyes aware and turned to the Cross, I could crucify that unreal expectation and adopt a tempered view of them. I choose to see them as God made them to be—fellow warriors becoming virtuous men.

———

To see others as God created them to be, and to choose not to conform them to my own misbegotten image: that was temperance. Parts of me that were underdeveloped, empty, or inclined to fill the void with homo-romantic fantasy began to fill out a bit. I gained new emotional muscle, new objectivity, and new discipline with which to be ordered to the world, to see things in truth. My fragile, often skewed sensibility became subject to reality and its Author.

Today, temperance prevails in my friendships. Yet this virtue's steady presence still requires engagement on my part. Bring it on, Jesus! I want to mirror another's divine image, not a diabolical one issuing from residual renegade desire.

We must make every effort to engage ourselves fully in the aspiration to temperance in friendship. How else can we truly be chaste—undivided, clear, and able to moderate our own desires in such a way that frees us to confirm another as God made him or her to be? In that way, we all have a hand at confirming another's ordered life or its disordering. I don't want to confuse or use another! Temperance frees us here; it helps us to acknowledge a range of responses to another, positive or negative.

I may be drawn to someone—find him or her physically attractive, emotionally appealing, or spiritually compelling. I acknowledge that response and choose not to come under shame for it. In fact, I take heart that I can recognize and respond to something that is good, true, or beautiful in another. To paraphrase Aquinas, "asexuality" is a greater defect than the good of desire.[141] Yet self-awareness invites choice. Given exuberant feelings, temperance frees me to make choices for another's good. That means neither objectifying nor slavishly devoting myself to him or her.

I take seriously St. James's condemnation of partiality (James 2:1–7). He urges us to show no favoritism to the sleek and the strong but rather to opt to serve the poor before the rich. In the work I do, I am always mindful of persons from disordered sexual

[141] Ibid., 154.

backgrounds who congregate only with the young and desirable; they pass over persons bearing more obvious brokenness in their identities. Temperance calls us to see with the eyes of our hearts and to serve persons whose beauty may be veiled, just waiting to be summoned by our service to them!

When I began trying to serve others, the Father, through the Spirit, helped me to exercise temperance in my efforts to help the disintegrated grow in chastity. I distrusted my rather vain desire to heed first the sleek and strong. I learned to listen to my heart when another's brokenness repulsed me. Instead of recoiling, I would ask myself: where did that young woman's hard, angry countenance come from? How much abuse has she suffered? What lack of fathering and persistent peer rejection has that extremely effeminate young man faced? Would I be another man in authority who looks at him with veiled scorn?

Ezekiel decries the shepherds who feed off the lovely sheep and refuse the strays—the lonely ones lost on that dark day (Ezek. 34: 5-12). The prophet champions their cure—the Good Shepherd who will pursue the most wounded and vulnerable. Temperance frees me to get in step with this Jesus who leaves the ninety-nine for the one (Luke 15:3-7). That can only occur when I deny my own need and behold another's greater need; temperance helps to rectify my vision when I am tempted to see only what pleases me and not what matters most to God. Growth in temperance has strengthened my capacity to love impartially.

Yet I am a weak man. And I dwell among people who have mistaken sexual needs for emotional needs; for them, love is hard to fathom without an element of seduction. What has kept me from falling? Temperance, yes; it helps me to moderate my desire for persons who may use their physical charms to rouse and compel me to pay special attention to them. I keep in mind constantly, daily, that I can be bought; my temperance is not so integrated that I am incapable of being seduced. I rely upon awareness of my own heightened response to another and the spirit of temperance that alerts me when my desires threaten to seep over the embankment that secures me in my marriage to both Annette and Jesus.

Neither looks kindly upon my cuddling up to the sheep. On a few occasions, Annette has pointed out my inordinate interest in ministry-related friends and has challenged me to straighten up a bit. That reminds me to release that person quickly to God and ask for the grace to behold Jesus over and under and around that person. He or she is not mine—One greater prevails. To impose possessive desire on the creature is to leech light from the Creator.

Here, temperance works in conjunction with holy fear: a holy fear of this God who calls me to serve impartially, combined with a high regard for this moral weakness that still has power to tank me if I forget.

———

First, let's look at the holy fear of God. My understanding of this is forged in an age that demonizes those of us who refuse to bend the knee to LGBT+ identification and who instead worship the God who calls them into something splendid: their integration as men and women.

We either fear the God who made us or bow before the "new normal." We are in a fight: our bodies, our desires, and our formation as persons are on the battlefield. Only the one who surrenders wholly to Jesus will make it through this narrow way. I like to think of it as a small but mighty crosscurrent coursing right up the middle of a polluted river. We catch that current when we offer ourselves fully to the One who reveals Himself as blood and water and spirit (1 John 5:6-8).

A long time ago, as a divided, intemperate young man, I bowed the knee to Jesus. I simply acknowledged that He was who He said He was and that I would follow His lead. He had proven Himself faithful to me. I believed Him. I had no idea what the future held, no clue to my sexual prognosis; I simply knew that He was the cure, and apart from Him, I had no way forward. I feared the Lord.

In that season of surrender, Fr. Alfred Delp's seeds about fear of God fell on good soil:

> Man must learn again—personally, actually, practically, daily—to reckon God as the ultimate category of reality, as the decisive judgment of all that exists. We have lost this category of godly fear. We are no longer a people of clarity who recognize this one Lord and who stand in simplicity without usurping the Lord's rights, and without betraying our duty to Him, or bargaining. Fear of God means knowing the absolute, inalienable dominion of the Lord of all.[142]

We align ourselves with the God who made us and who is redeeming us as we look to Him and Him alone. The beautiful thing about our countercultural devotion is that the lines are crystal clear. We pick up our little crosses and follow Him—denying what feels good to us in order to align with the truth. Unlike many who sputter about in "normal" compromises that dull them but don't quite drown them, we may feel to be on the brink of engulfment frequently. We cling to Him, our anchor, sure and steadfast (Heb. 6:19). To let go and gain the world would cost us our very souls.

---

[142] Alfred Delp, *Advent of the Heart*, 127.

This is holy fear, marked by the Cross. It is complemented by a high regard for the sin that could disintegrate us.

———

When our ordered selves are challenged by disordered passions, we invoke the name above all names, which secures what seems to be our slippery grasp on temperance. This Jesus reaches to our depths with tender mercies; He towers over other gods. We surrender afresh, aware that we could be swept out to sea. Yet He is faithful to help the helpless who cry out to Him. In Pieper's words, "fear guards the summit of our hope", this Jesus to whom we could be lost but who will not let us go.[143]

Pieper combines temperance and holy fear:

> Even the Holy Spirit's gift of fear, which St. Thomas assigns to *temperantia* [temperance], purifies the soul by causing it to experience, through grace, the innermost peril of man. Its fruit is that purity by dint of which the selfish and furtive search for spurious fulfillment is abandoned. Purity is the perfect unfolding of the whole nature from which could have come the words: "Behold the handmaid of the Lord!" (Luke 1:38).
>
> A new depth opens here to our view: purity is not only the fruit of purification, it implies at the same time readiness to accept God's purifying intervention, terrible and fatal though it might be; to accept it with bold candor of a trustful heart, and thus to experience its fruitful and transforming power.[144]

---

[143] Pieper, *Faith, Hope, Love*, 138.
[144] Pieper, *The Four Cardinal Virtues*, 205–206.

A pastor friend of mine, Bill, had a deep and compassionate heart, yet he was intemperate, blind to his mixed motives with attractive women. He would zero in on their deep need for a father's love, and they would nurture devotion to him. Now dependent on confusing Pastor Bill, the woman would become infatuated and enter the dance of sexual immorality with him.

One relationship woke him up. He saw for the first time the hell he was imposing on this woman and then could see the others who had preceded her. He saw the depth of his divided heart for the first time. God, in His mercy, gave him the gift of holy fear: the truth that he could be lost to God through seducing little ones into sinful acts that warrant death (Mark 9:42). He submitted to a long break from ministry and guided counsel in order to sit in the reality of his sin and choose to die to it.

He did months of "cross-time": identifying with Jesus in His death "attaining to the resurrection from the dead" (Phil. 3:10–11). Not only did he need "to abandon the selfish and furtive search for spurious fulfillment," he needed to have those motives burned out of him through death, through an identification with Christ Crucified.[145] Pastor Bill claims that he hung on that cross for a long time; that alone effected the purification born of holy fear. He vows today never to return to that slippery, divided place again. I believe him. He talks about his painful history; he tells on himself; the light of almighty mercy burns off shame and banishes the shadows that beckon still. He boasts in the Cross and thus glorifies the One who never let him go.

Pastor Bill cares for others now in a tempered way. He is becoming chaste. A subset of temperance, chastity orders the uniquely sexual dimension of our humanity to the whole of us,

[145] Ibid., 205.

with special attention to our spirituality. It has everything to do with growth in personal integrity—ordering the person into sexual wholeness—thereby ensuring that we offer a whole gift to others.[146] Through growth in chastity, we can aspire to offer ourselves to others in the spirit of Jesus' self-giving, a gift of which we need not be ashamed.

Here Pieper helps us by asserting the good of sexual desire. He reminds us to see the "fulfillment of the natural sexual urge and its pleasure as good and not in the least sinful, assuming order and moderation are preserved."[147] Sex preserves us—it is essential to all living; its necessity and our tendency to lust means we must make every effort to preserve its order.[148] Chastity rightly disciplines our sexuality and guides the streams of life in a creative and loving direction.[149]

Full and fruitful sexual expression occurs only in marriage. The *Catechism* describes sexuality as "personal and truly human when it is integrated into the relationship of one person to another, in the complete and lifelong mutual gift of a man and a woman."[150] Pieper elaborates on this commitment when he says that "marriage is the proper fulfillment of sexual power" and involves a community of life and offspring, as well as sacramental blessing.[151] He especially highlights marriage as "community of life"; here we see an inner logic, brought out later by Pope St. Paul VI in *Humane Vitae*, which necessitates openness to children and a lifetime vow between man and wife to help order the lives created.

---

[146] Ibid., 163.
[147] Ibid., 154.
[148] Ibid., 155.
[149] Ibid., 155.
[150] *Catechism of the Catholic Church*, 2337.
[151] Pieper, *The Four Cardinal Virtues*, 158.

Rediscovering Our Lost Fullness

As a convert from a sexually divided background, I celebrate the openness and the vow. Sex must give an answer for itself. Having overflowed the banks and damaged others in the turbulence, I became secure in my sexual "purpose" only with the help of chastity and its goal of fruitfulness. My body is created to beget life! Chastity rescues sex from being just a gymnastic exercise. But it also rescues us from total abstinence. Chastity liberates sex to give life and to order the sexes to tend to that life. Through chastity, we integrate our powers of life and love so we can fulfill our human destiny to be at once fruitful and responsible.

What astounds me is how my wife and I, after over forty years, tend to that life more than ever: in appropriate guidance to adult kids and blessedly messy care of grandkids. Little did I know, when our bodies first fused exuberantly, that we would fire up and burn on all cylinders in order to shepherd an entire community of Comiskeys. Family life doesn't lessen as Annette and I gray; it expands and deepens. It necessitates more and not less of the virtue of chastity. Our ever-expanding brood deserves the integrity of our gift to each other and to them.

For sustained integrity, I am grateful for examples and walking partners like Mike and Diane; their witness spurs me on. And I am grateful to the Catholic Church for her moral teaching on chastity, both in singleness and in marriage.

———

Perhaps that helps explain my outrage over compromises taking root in worldly Christians that block this progress toward fruitfulness. As LGBT+ ideology has converted lives throughout the West, I notice that some members of the Church have acclimated to a static notion of gender diversity in her members. Weak caregivers confirm Christ-seekers who have been socialized by rainbow anthropology as "gay" or "trans" or "undecided." It grieves me that some church guides support a generation's wandering in a barren land.

Fr. James Martin validates a decidedly unchaste way of building a bridge to the LGBT+ community when he says: "A name in Hebrew Scriptures stands for a person's identity.... Let's listen to what our gay and lesbian sisters and transgender siblings prefer to name themselves."[152] He bases his point on scriptural accounts of naming transactions. But there, the Creator names the creature; in Martin's gospel, we name ourselves according to man-made constructs and in rebellion from God's will for our humanity.

Chastity refuses this! This virtue insists on integration with our biological selves, a process of reconciliation with the gendered gift we are. That, of course, has a myriad of psychological and spiritual implications. These become apparent to each fractured soul as he or she pilgrims to wholeness. Quoting St. Augustine, the *Catechism* claims that "through chastity we are gathered back together and led back to the unity from which we were fragmented into multiplicity."[153] The man who split off from the good of his manhood is invited by the spirit of chastity to unite with his own gender gift. The woman divided by wounded men and inclined to the refuge of her own gender unites with the "one who holds all things together" (Col. 1:17). He has unique authority to reconcile her back to herself, from brokenness to wholeness, by "making peace through his blood, shed on the cross" (Col. 1:20).

Here we reckon with chastity as a goal and a gift. Though requiring effort, it is "a grace.... The Holy Spirit enables one

---

[152] James Martin, *Building a Bridge: How the Catholic Church and the LGBT Community Can Enter Into a Relationship of Respect, Compassion, and Sensitivity* (New York: HarperCollins Publishers, 2017), 23–24.
[153] *Catechism of the Catholic Church*, 2340.

whom the water of Baptism has regenerated to imitate the purity of Christ."[154] That same Spirit empowers us to accept chastity as a lifelong journey—"a long and exacting" road that cannot be acquired once and for all, and "presupposes renewed effort at all stages of life."[155] I love that: it means I am chaste and I am becoming chaste; I am more whole today than yesterday, confident that the fractures that still flare are lessening with each step.

Pieper masterfully points out how chastity enables us to reason well in the sexual arena. I can attest to this. As I abstained from obvious sexual sins and grew in self-control, I began to see "trees walking," like the partially healed blind man at Bethsaida (Mark 8:22-26). Then, as I grew in temperance and began to integrate more of my true humanity, I beheld as blessed this gift of man for woman and woman for man. And I began to want it! Operating under temperance and involving this self-control, chastity unblocked in me passageways of divine energy.[156] In fits and starts, my sexual waters began to flow toward women and one woman in particular. Just as prudence—seeing things as they actually are—guides chastity, so did becoming chaste help me see reality more clearly.[157] Growth in chastity also freed me to act reasonably upon what I saw.

"Without a direct, innocent, and selfless vision of reality, there can be no interior order of the moral person and no honest moral decision."[158] On the other hand, says Pieper: "To be open to the truth of real things and to live by the truth that one has grasped is the essence of the moral being. Only when

---

[154] Ibid., 2345.
[155] Ibid., 2342.
[156] Pieper, *The Four Cardinal Virtues*, 163.
[157] Ibid., 205.
[158] Ibid., 162.

we recognize the state of things can we likewise understand the depths to which the unchaste heart permits destruction to invade its very being."[159]

———

That's why St. Paul warns us that sexual sin is distinct in its profound capacity to self-violate, a sin against self that divides one's integrity (1 Cor. 6:12–20). Pieper seconds this: "Unchastity begets a blindness of spirit ... which splits the power of decision."[160] He cautions us that sins against chastity (the Catechism gives us quite a range—lust and fornication, porn and masturbation, homosexuality)[161] make us unreasonable. That can be disastrous: if you are a divided, lustful soul, you tend neither to see truth clearly nor to act prudently and decisively. In the end, you will treat others badly, unjustly, not giving them their due.

Pornography is unique in its power to skew reality and relinquish the self to a fake universe that renders a person unable and unwilling to deal with his or her actual world. Here one is "enkindled above all by the seductive glamour of the stimuli provided in an artificial civilization, with which the dishonorable team of blind lust and calculated greed surround the province of sexuality."[162] I have walked with countless persons of both sexes weaned on fake video intimacy framed in fake seductive scenarios. The impact: a splitting of their gift within—bowed down by shame and despair over an unquenchable desire for yet another clip, which contributes to a divided vision without. Not only are real people, including

---

[159] Ibid.
[160] Ibid., 159–160.
[161] *Catechism of the Catholic Church*, 2351–2359.
[162] Pieper, *The Four Cardinal Virtues*, 149.

spouses, nothing like the sexy idols on film, but strangers who intersect physically with one's video lovers become targets of desire and even sexual conquest.

That is the demonic power of porn; it splits our best knowledge about sexuality: that real desire emerges out of loving a whole person. Porn disengages us from persons and poisons us with arousal for phantoms. Unlike any other drug, porn fuels what Aquinas describes as "the roaming unrest of spirit."[163] Under its influence, we cannot see or feel clearly. We tremble like a devotee of Baal, dancing frantically and driven only by our pleasure (1 Kings 18:26–29). "An unchaste man wants above all something for himself ... his constantly strained will-to-pleasure prevents him from confronting reality with that selfless detachment which makes genuine knowledge possible... The destructiveness of this disorder lies in the fact that it stifles the power of perceiving reality."[164]

Leanne Payne warns us of the unrealities we foster in our hearts:

> An unhealthy fantasy life is a killer. It destroys. It wars against and annihilates the true imagination, that which can intuit the real and is therefore creative. When our minds are pregnant with illusion, with the lie that disintegrates the personality, and our eyes are set on this, we cannot be impregnated by that which is true and substantive—that which unites the personality and makes it one.[165]

Unchaste fantasies divide and conquer us; clinging to worthless idols, "we forfeit the grace that could be [ours]" (Jonah 2:8).

---

[163] Ibid., 200.
[164] Ibid., 161.
[165] Leanne Payne, *Healing Presence* (Westchester: Crossways Books, 1989), 121.

I will tell one last example of the unrealities wrought by unchastity and the hope that temperance brings through almighty mercy. Kim, a good friend of mine, struggled with same-sex attraction during her marriage. The more stress she experienced as a mother of three young children, the more she craved a woman who would take care of her. A woman she met online connected with this craving, and when they met, she felt "born again," as if all her needs and desires culminated in this person. No one else knew her struggles or her temptations, which had been fanned into flame by a world hell-bent on urging her "out" and into adultery. She needed help but sought none. Instead of the *Catechism*, which stresses cultural structures that support formation in chastity,[166] Kim had been socialized by media-driven fantasies of the perfect female partner. The fire to burn bridges with her husband and children ignited years before as she conjured lovers on the sly.

Unreality. No one could believe she abandoned her family. She had evidently loved her kids. And her husband. Yet the stimulus of this other woman swelled her "waters" into waves that crashed over every bank she held dear, including her faith. Unchastity invited her into the dream that quickly became a nightmare: her new friend proved unstable and left her after six months. Alone, she came to her senses. The spirit of temperance gently began to woo her back to the One who could order her once again, and, in a way, for the first time. Her adultery did not begin with the one affair. It started years earlier in deep, unexpressed longing that she nurtured alone. Kim turned and wordlessly invoked mercy. She allowed the Father to run to her as she staggered home. She felt

---

[166] *Catechism of the Catholic Church*, 2344.

His embrace and the godly fear that she could have lost everything to an illusion, an unreality.

Pieper writes: "One who rejects fulfillment in its true and final meaning ... may well regard the artificial paradise of unrestrained pleasure-seeking as the sole place, if not of happiness, then of forgetfulness, of self-oblivion."[167] In turning to God, Kim came face-to-face with herself. She began slowly to reengage with reality through a good pastor and counselor who helped her to sorrow over sin and rebuild the bridge to her family. But this time, she did it as a woman with historic divides who needed to struggle in the light of trusted others.

She humbled herself and got involved in a Living Waters group, where she began to walk with others alongside and toward Jesus; she discovered that she could address unmet needs in her life without sin and responsibly serve persons who needed her. Hail, holy spirit of temperance! This most personal of virtues helped Kim tend to the cry of her "inner child" while caring for the real children for whom she was responsible.

Mercy kisses temperance here. While the former frees us to resume the journey toward chastity and the holy ordering of our desires, temperance preserves and defends that order in us; "it creates the indispensable prerequisite for both the realization of the actual good and the actual movement of man toward his goal."[168] Today Kim walks as a wife and mother with a slight limp, "sorrowful, yet always rejoicing," as she journeys home (2 Cor. 6:10).

How beautiful is the fruit of temperance for those of us whose hearts have been blinded and divided by unchastity. I rejoice that my eyes are open and remain open to behold the beauty of all God has given me in Annette. Our cure is simple but time-consuming

[167] Pieper, *The Four Cardinal Virtues*, 204.
[168] Ibid., 175.

and constant. Every effort is worth it. To arise through mercy before the One who looks on us with almighty tenderness, to catch His gaze with increasingly pure eyes, to savor His sweetness: this is our cure and our goal! This is temperance.

Beneath the overcoming of specific unchaste habits, we discover holy intimacy. Temperance is the virtue that enables us to squander ourselves in loving Him and so discover He has been waiting to love us, simply, deeply, only. Only eyes made pure can see; "only he who is silent can hear."[169] Gerald May points out succinctly that "addicted people can't meditate."[170] But as we surrender our divided, agitated selves to the only One who can make us whole, He invites us to participate in becoming whole. We learn to quiet ourselves and discover, in the words of Robert Cardinal Sarah, that "silence is not an absence ... it manifests the most intense of all presences."[171] Temperance helps us to cultivate a profound capacity to contemplate the beauty of the Lord.

In His Presence, and particularly in Eucharistic Adoration, we learn to worship wordlessly the One who is above all yet is tenderly near to us. I say with assurance that adoration has become my lifeline that nourishes a composed and docile spirit. Fixed upon the God who gave all to gain me, now contained in breathtaking humility in the Host, I behold Beauty. That frees me to extract what is beautiful from a broken world, to cultivate "a chaste sensuality that can realize the faculty of perceiving beauty and to enjoy it for its sake, undeterred by the self-centered will to pleasure ... only those who look at the world with pure eyes can experience its beauty."[172]

---

[169] Ibid., 161.

[170] Gerald May, *Addiction and Grace: Love and Spirituality in the Healing of Addictions* (New York: HarperCollins, 1988), 44.

[171] Cardinal Robert Sarah, *The Power of Silence*, 27.

[172] Pieper, *The Four Cardinal Virtues*, 167.

Temperance guards and goads me as I grow into one who, through the Creator, can behold the beauty of His creatures. No small thing for someone cut deeply by broken images! Yet what is true remains, and He calls my name, over and over, and condescends to make Himself evident to me. Not content for me to merely avoid trouble, He frees me to peer through the wilderness to see gardens, to regard one whom I might have reduced to an object and now can honor as a whole person. Temperance orders our passions so weak ones like me can relate chastely to loved ones and to a beautiful, but broken world.

ELEVEN

Liberating Chastity

"Christ loved the Church and gave Himself up for her" (Eph. 5:25). I can grow in chastity because its author and finisher lives within me. I am never alone in my quest to become whole. The good work of integration He started in me He will finish.

Our understanding of chastity is rightly framed by other virtues over which Jesus prevails. Is He not the master of prudence, the very Source of Reality who acts decisively on the basis of what is, discerning even the suspicious thoughts of the Pharisee toward the sinful woman (Luke 7:39)? And does He not serve justice—giving every one of us our due—just as He did with the woman caught in adultery and with her accusers (John 8:1-11)? He embodied fortitude as He blazed a trail to Jerusalem (Luke 9:51), and there He remained brave amid a host of murderers. With each disciple, He exercised temperance, ordering His intense desire for their good by continually inviting them to become better, as when He cast one sorrowful glance at Peter, thereby prompting swift repentance after the apostle's third denial (Luke 22:61).

Chaste Jesus. I love how His longing to connect with men and women alike was tender and strong. Free from both lust and rigorous self-concern, He offered Himself wholly to others. No other way to explain the decisive yet winsome way He loved the most shamed and sexually vulnerable. Think of the Samaritan woman who would have forever turned her gaze from Him had He not tuned in to her deepest need. I contend that something lean and virile and quietly powerful emanated from Him; He exercised mastery over his bodily longings in order to love people clearly and well.

Okay, admittedly, virtuous Jesus is a tough act to follow. But He helps us. We become like Him through Him.

And that's why we need God in order to represent Him well. Nothing could be more deeply personal than the powers of life and love—but the stream of His life-giving love for us runs deeper still and has power to help us to direct our passions for the good.

That requires a deeper relationship with Jesus than with our sensational and often disturbing sexual desires. We cannot grow in chastity if we are more aware of our disordered interiority than we are of Him who loves us and who may not be as shocked as we are.

I laugh a little at how startled I am by flashes of old idols; all the while, He looks at me lovingly, simply waiting for a chance just to care for me. I spend way too much time wondering "why." All He wants is for me to fix my eyes on Him. Therein lies His power to whisk away any intrusion so He can quiet my agitated heart.

I recall a wonderful man in one of my groups who was rigorously Catholic. He could not have been more disciplined and conscientious—and yet he could not have been *less* sure of the Father's love. He always felt like he was working hard to be loved but never quite made it. About midway through the group, he realized that he had no personal relationship with Jesus. He admitted: "I believed my brokenness disqualified me from God; I distanced myself and tried to get better for God. Now I realize He wants to love me; He wants to love me into chastity." Though he barely knew how to welcome that love, he rejoiced that he found his cure—the Father's love, revealed in Jesus. He declared happily: "I've not known this God whom I have sought. But now I do, just a little, and that gives me great hope. I want to know Him more."

That's why, when we gather, we always focus on St. Faustina's Divine Mercy image. Nothing brings us nearer to the love that makes us chaste than the fruit of His Cross. In one glance, we are reminded: "O Blood and Water, which gushed forth from the Heart of Jesus as a fount of Mercy for us, I trust in You!" Through our eyes, each heart can behold and confirm that Jesus ecstatically loves us. My take on the Divine Mercy? "My beloved is mine and I am his" (Song of Sol. 2:16).

Ecstasy is the only word that will do. On the Cross, Jesus came out of Himself (*ex-stasis*, Greek for "out of one's being") by releasing His whole life for our divided lives. St. John described Blood and water as the first evident fruit of Jesus' death (John 19:34): He poured out His Blood so it might transfuse ours, and He poured out water in order to baptize us into a new creation.

That river keeps flowing to cleanse and heal us as we new creations stumble *en route* to greater chastity. I may falter, but now my heart is far more inclined toward merciful Jesus than to sexy idols. I fall *forward*, and His Cross confirms His exchange of my shame for His double portion of favor (Isa. 61:7). Pretty good deal: in the face of the Cross, weakness becomes an occasion for further integration.

I always understand Jesus' radical self-giving as the flood that frees me to love Annette ecstatically. Just as my personal integrity hinges on Jesus' self-giving on the Cross, so my interpersonal integrity finds depth and meaning in giving myself to her. Again, we return to "ecstasy," only this time in Hebrew and used to describe the "deep sleep" (Gen. 2:21) that came upon Adam in preparation for the rib removed from his body (out-of-body indeed!) the rib from which God made Eve. Jesus takes the Pharisees back to this vision in Matthew 19:4–6 to show them why man and woman discover an original unity when they come together as one flesh. We two, who have become one, give ourselves in a way that prophesies the self-giving of Jesus. I give myself to her, and she becomes my bride: Jesus gives all and creates for Himself a Bride: the Church.

The Church. The life-giving flood released on the Cross births not merely the individual Christian, but the Church united and composed of many members. St. Augustine distilled this truth when he said: "As Eve came forth from the side of the sleeping Adam, the Church was born from the side of the suffering Christ";[173] "the Second Adam bowed His Head and fell asleep at the Cross, that a spouse may be formed for Him from that which flowed from the sleeper's side. O death, whereby the dead are raised to life! What can be purer than such blood? What more health-giving than such a wound?"[174]

I love that. From Jesus' wound came a Bride whom He treasured as His own, a chaste Bride undivided in devotion and whole in self-giving, one to another. Chastity necessitates being rightly knit into communion with each other. I know now that I cannot be chaste unless I take my place among the members of Jesus.

---

[173] Brant Pitre, *Jesus the Bridegroom: The Greatest Love Story Ever Told* (New York: Crown Publishing Group, 2014), 111.

[174] Augustine, "Tractate CXX on the Gospel of John," trans. John Gibb in *Nicene and Post-Nicene Fathers, First Series*, vol. 7, ed. Phillip Schaff (New York: Christian Literature Publishing, 1888), 435.

I had always ached for that communion. And I experienced a form of healing solidarity in a host of "free churches" where we would gather in humility and discover the Cross in our disclosures, one to another. Still, the upheavals in my evangelical, charismatic world due to large personalities and varied interpretations divided me. The wholeness of my temple required something more. I could work out personal integrity only so far without reckoning more deeply with the greater temple, the Church of Jesus Christ.

I discovered the communion of the saints. Yes, that included the somewhat remote souls with whom I shared pews at Mass, connecting limply with a "passing of the peace" and a race out to the crowded parking lot. But in the leanness, the long season of gaining enough traction to be known as a sinner among a few, I realized something deeper was holding us together. Centuries of faithful ones, united by the line of Peter, who now in Heaven cry out for us on earth; they "fix the whole Church more firmly in holiness.... So by their fraternal concern is our weakness greatly helped."[175]

I was lonely but not alone. Looking out at my large parish, I realized that we were woven together by golden threads spun through centuries of heavenly intercession. Connection was profound if not yet socially realized. This freed me. As the English mystic Caryll Houselander wrote, "Realization of our oneness in Christ is the only cure for human loneliness.... For me, the greatest joy in being once again in full communion with the Catholic Church has been, and is now, the ever-growing reassurance given by the Mystical Body of Christ ... and that Christ and His Church are one."[176]

---

[175] *Catechism of the Catholic Church*, 956.

[176] Caryll Houselander, "Reconciled in Christ," in *Magnificat* (March 2020), 85–86.

An unseen prayer choir elevated me in the absence of human encouragement. I lost a lot of connections from familiar sources: friends who, for a host of reasons, distrusted the Church and me in it. None of my family of origin, nor the one I fathered, followed me into the Church (my daughter Katie, bless her, did some years later). That was especially painful for Annette. In good conscience, she could not launch into Catholicism, and that remains a deep wound for us, and especially for her. We had always shared our lives in one community of devotion and service. Now we labor and eat at separate tables: a divide not deep enough to sever our unity in Christ and one-flesh commitment, but strong enough to cast us upon Jesus' mercy.

I found solidarity with the saints; it was as if they cheered me onward and made little rejections sweet occasions for deeper communion with Jesus. Once, I wept deeply for an hour or so over the loss of several fine ministry friends. I sensed a blue mantle being placed over my shoulders and later realized that Mary was interceding for me. As "she is the 'exemplary realization' (typus) of the Church,"[177] she somehow was present to extend consolation to me. Amazing.

I lost no ground in chastity in this tearing season. Perhaps I gained some, learning to linger longer in His presence before the altar, under the Crucified. I felt surrounded in a way I had never experienced. *That* is communion, being knit together with all His members, including those heavenly ones who pray for me as I endure little losses while seeking to love Jesus' members more wholly.

That included my wife, who bled as a result of my conversion to Catholicism. Perhaps this prophesied something of the bleeding hearts of Jesus and Mary over the divided Church. And rather than pontificate over the "flawless" community I discovered as a

---

[177] *Catechism of the Catholic Church*, 967.

Catholic, I admit disappointment. To be sure, I discovered a host of blessed and committed members, but they were offset by others who, though baptized, had yet to break the worldly spell still enchanting them. Inconsistent and syncretistic, these lukewarm ones reminded me of the members of the Church of Thyatira, captivated by false teachers who "misleads [Jesus'] servants into sexual immorality" (Rev. 2:20), and the Church at Laodicea, whose bourgeois members, though spiritually crippled, failed to recognized their need to be saved at all (Rev. 3:17–18).

Sadly, I encountered many priests who failed to represent Jesus in the area of chastity. I cannot know for sure why. A few looked askance at me when I witnessed as to what Jesus had done in my life; they claimed that Jesus did not transform persons with same-sex attraction—one should just accommodate its stubbornness. Others responded confusedly upon hearing my confessions that one should just accept his "weakness." I could not help speculating as to whether some of these men had entered the priesthood in part due to their own sexual conflicts. Were they now, as fathers, passing on their "empty way of life" (1 Pet. 1:18) to their spiritual children?

Our divides as a Church are deep. I'm a sinner, and I'm grateful for any progress I have made in chastity. So I cast no stone but rather grieve over the cradle Catholics around me: those who are poorly formed morally, unaware of the depths of their divides, and who don't yet know this Jesus who could set them free. Perhaps shame repels mercy. Vaguely anxious, they value their "tradition" yet realize things aren't as they should be. They don't know how to access the grace that could be theirs.

The best metaphor I know for us as a Church today is the Samaritan woman. Contrary to popular belief, the Samaritan woman was religiously devout and proud. A beleaguered people,

Samaritans had historically worshipped the God of Israel but had been overtaken by the Canaanites, who compelled them to worship at different altars.[178] "They worshipped the Lord, but they also served their own gods" (2 Kings 17:33). Such idolatry led to immorality, as the Samaritans devoted themselves to pagan deities, often through sexual orgies. Divided faith, divided bodies. They were seriously shamed by the Jews, who held them in contempt for their historic compromises. On the one hand, a proud and tough ethos—the defiant face—on the other, a face aware of compromise, looking down, covered in shame.

That Samaritan woman is us! The Catholic theologian Brant Pitre asserts that the Samaritan woman represents the people of God: many members forming the mosaic of a Bride, whose evident need of her Bridegroom is present in us all.[179] I concur. Most Catholics have not lost the true good of their inheritance but have simply become cluttered by worldly debris. For this we feel ashamed, but we don't know how to get back to the garden.

Just as He did with the Samaritan woman, Jesus encounters us winsomely with our human need for dignity and kindness (John 4:7-9), and with our deepest longing: (living water—liquid love), the spirit of mercy springs up in us and quenches our thirst forever (John 4:13-14). His merciful presence gently erodes our coat of shame and engages our hearts' desire for holy love. Mercy Himself peers tenderly into our eyes and exposes our divided hearts, our multiple lovers and altars; He invites us into unity through worship of the One. One Love; one Cross flowing freely with "living water"; one table where He satisfies our desires with good things; one people from a host of backgrounds who now unite under the

---

[178] Pitre, *Jesus the Bridegroom*, 63.
[179] Ibid., 80.

Cross, through mercy. "Once you were not a people, but now you are the people of God; once you had not received mercy, but now you have received mercy" (1 Pet. 2:10).

Mercy makes the way for the divided Bride to become one—one gentle exposure, one fresh washing, one encouragement, one meal after another. The fruit is a chaste Bride for whom Jesus is returning. It's like you want to say on the day: "My entire being—body, soul, and spirit—exclaims Holy, Holy, Holy is the Lord Almighty; no other gods before You!"

Chastity. I love how merciful Jesus makes a way for us to grow in this exquisite virtue. Accompanied by Him and His friends, we learn how to navigate what appears in the world to be a disappearing path. Underneath the weeds and thorns, the way to integration remains true. It is simply up to us to behold the One who goes before us; as we walk, our eyes fixed on Him, we clear that path for pilgrims yet to come. Just like the Samaritan woman, we tell others the wonders He has done (John 4:28-30). We find new walking partners for the adventure of a lifetime.

——

So after all this, I hope you see why I think chastity is freedom. I'll leave you with a few final encouragements about chastity.

First, chastity frees us to win the war of words. I am convinced that chastity is the single best definition of sexual and relational wholeness. Though often misunderstood as "Catholic abstinence," chastity encompasses a dimensional understanding of what it means to be human in our passions. Chastity is about ordering our passions so that the powers of life and love give rise to life rather than squander it. That involves a dozen little streams that contribute to a creative river teeming with life, yet necessarily cleansed, stirred, and directed for the *sake* of life. These smaller streams include reconciliation to one's birth gender, cultivating self-awareness so that one's sexual inclinations remain under the sway of a deft will, setting boundaries with persons of interest, and growing in respect and insight for one's desires.

However mysterious this river is, it is informed by wisdom that liberates sexual integration. Chastity frees us to rejoice in the good gift that we are and are becoming.

When we wise up to what chastity is, we win. We no longer confuse anyone with LGBT+ language. We are simply moving toward God's goal for every man and woman: chastity, the integration of who we are—male and female made in His image. Chastity silences "gay versus straight" chatter, "heterosexual versus homosexual" jargon. We are simply men and women becoming chaste.

We win the messy culture battles concerning "reparative" therapy and the question: "Can the homosexual change?" There is no "homosexual" in God's anthropology. There are only persons with certain vulnerabilities, much loved by Jesus. And "reparative therapy," a term coined by Dr. Joseph Nicolosi, is simply a tool for understanding how some persons, especially males, become disintegrated in their sexual selves.[180] The goal remains chastity, and one should be free to pursue whatever course of clinical and pastoral action one desires in the quest to become a more integrated person.

Jesus is the author and finisher of chastity; He, not a particular treatment, is our goal. We seek first His glorious Kingdom (Matt. 6:33), and He adds to us the ordering of our desires. Chastity has many faces: it's at once psychological and spiritual, cognitive and passionate, restrained and exuberant.

---

[180] Joseph Nicolosi, *Reparative Therapy of Male Homosexuality: A New Clinical Approach* (Lanham: Rowman and Littlefield Publishers, 1991).

The Catholic Church must maximize her inheritance here; we can and will "raise up the age-old foundations" (Isa. 58:12) related to the gift of chastity. Moral theologians must not stammer here but with acuity cast vision for us all; pastors must heed these words and take seriously Jesus' high, earthy call on them to embody integrity.

And seminary formators must ensure, as marvelous Kenrick-Glennon Seminary in St. Louis does, that candidates for the priesthood reveal who they are and how they are working out their sexual integrity. One cannot renounce natural fatherhood for the Kingdom if one hasn't a desire for it. "Reveal yourself!" must become the credo for all men aspiring to today's priesthood. For too long we have tolerated persons cloaking their sexual frustrations with a celibate "call." We need fathers who are working the program—engaging with God and each other honestly *en route* to robust, virile chastity.

Secondly, chastity insists on a trajectory of wholeness for all pilgrims. There is no end, just growing integration until we see Him face-to-face. Chastity frees us from disparaging our progress in ordering desire. We should not, and indeed *cannot*, claim absolute wholeness. That belies our still fallen state. Disordered desire lessens and is redirected, but the heart's ragged edges are still there. Newness of life frees us to see the dirt and call it what it is, thereby taking ground in chastity and reflecting Him a little more fully, one day at a time.

Thirdly, we tread the chaste path for a lifetime, but that does not mean we do not expect miracles! Do not forget that we walk with Jesus who helps us in our weakness and will surprise us with little graces that clear the path, especially by healing slow-bleeding wounds that impede chastity.

In one area of sexual conflict, I was handed by Jesus a small radiant cross. I discerned that He said to me: "Grasp this whenever that fear grips you and I will set you free." He freed me as I obeyed Him and grasped that cross. That conflict is now under the authority of Jesus. I am free of that fear.

On the path, He is mighty in power to free us and to keep us free. As this involves moral maturation, we have a hand in cooperating with His directives for our chastity. He gives us the dignity of ongoing choice as to whether we will take the next steps in our integration. There is always more integration because there is always more of Jesus to discover: more mercy that unblocks us and frees us to aspire to what would have been unimaginable to us months earlier. He is always present in love to help us to take the next steps. Because of Jesus, I have hope for every divided soul. No divide is too great for the marvel of His mercy.

Fourth, on chaste, solid ground, the Catholic Church must resist the worldly pull to assimilate LGBT+ "reality." Heed the demise of historic Protestantism in America! Whenever one of these once proud denominations, beginning with the Episcopalians, shook hands with LGBT+ activists and began to ordain "gay" clergy or perform "gay weddings," their death knell was assured. Each "gay-affirming" Protestant group in America is in free fall. Such compromise signals corruption within and a diluted, feel-good gospel held out to the world.

Most seekers do not want validation for their compromised lives; they want strong medicine. We seek the Savior because we know we need salvaging, not placating. When the Church dulls her moral clarity in order to gain the "world," she loses both the world and her own soul. People do not buy a discounted Gospel, and Jesus won't tolerate a Church that prostitutes herself to gain the divided. Heed this, Church: we embrace the divided, turn together, and proceed toward wholeness.

Fifth, chastity must involve walking partners. We become chaste together, with our priests, our counselors, and most importantly, with Christian friends on whom we learn to rely as we encourage one another in chastity. We as the Church of Jesus Christ must learn to tap into the profound and powerful resource of the "one another" in our common quest for integration. This is our greatest need. We know little about the beauty of chastity because we rarely hear witnesses of real people with broken lives whom Jesus met and integrated into a life-giving community. Instead, we hear horror stories of demonized fathers messing with innocents. We can do better, Church.

We counter the wickedness of a minuscule percentage by appropriately and candidly witnessing to how Jesus and His Church transformed our lives. Let's tell the good news about chastity! We who once squandered life and now create and protect it need to tell others. We who, like the Samaritan, thirsted and welcomed Jesus' offering us "living water" must release "rivers of living water" from within" (John 7:37–38). Spring up, O well, in exuberant praise of Jesus and the lives He is making chaste!

Perhaps we suffer from too low an expectation of what Jesus can do. He elevates our vision as we who share Jesus at the table also gather to reveal our deep need for this Savior and the community of His friends. We walk together for a while; we shed shame, invite mercy into wounds, and seek the help of one another in overcoming deep patterns of sin.

Gatherings like these in no way displace the sacramental forgiveness of the priest. But I can say with assurance that one priest cannot be solely responsible for helping a parish full of Jesus' divided members become whole. The needs are too great, the stakes of human dignity too high, the desire of Jesus for a chaste Bride too passionate for us not to mobilize the lay priesthood to accompany fellow sufferers.

Rediscovering Our Lost Fullness

At every Mass, we tell the whole congregation, "I confess to Almighty God, and to you, my brothers and sisters, that I have greatly sinned." Then we invoke the help of those brothers and sisters: "therefore I ask ... you, my brothers and sisters, to pray for me to the Lord our God."[181]

Got it. I believe it. Let's do it: "To you, my brothers and sisters, I will learn to reveal myself responsibly so that the greater authority of this one Body might rest upon me and become an antidote to my chastity, even as I, a member in good standing, advocate for yours."

From the very beginning of my Catholic life, over a decade ago, I prayed to integrate breaking bread with my Eucharistic family and breaking open our still-divided lives, one to another. Starting one Lent, a small group of us prayed every week for the chastity of our Church, beginning with our need for greater wholeness. People came in fits and starts: each one came from diverse backgrounds and was treated with the utmost dignity. Finally, our pastors gave the go-ahead for our core team to run a full Living Waters group.

During the group's initial run in the parish, I recall waiting in line for the Eucharist one Sunday morning. I looked ahead of me and saw several of my Living Waters friends and fellow Catholics: Linda, a beautiful woman facing unwanted singleness and a spirit of rejection because of it; Deacon Jim, seeking to overcome porn addiction; Sara and Bill, whose daughter had just "come out" as "gay"; Christopher, who as a teen had been abused by a pastor; Karen and Jim, whose marriage had been frustrated by the sexual baggage both brought into the relationship.

We, like the Samaritan, endured shame for the joy of Real Food, Jesus Himself. We quietly blessed each other as we ate. We took heart: we were not alone in our efforts to become chaste for Jesus

---

[181] From the "Confiteor" of the Roman Liturgy.

and for each other. Starting with our own lives, we were helping to prepare a Bride for Jesus without spot or wrinkle.

"Christ loved the church and gave himself up for her to make her holy, cleansing her by the washing of water with the word, and to present her to himself as a radiant church, without stain or wrinkle or any blemish, but holy and blameless" (Eph. 5:25–27).

About the Author

Andrew Comiskey, M.Div., has worked extensively with the healing of the sexually and relationally broken. He is director of Desert Stream/Living Waters Ministries (which he founded in 1980), a multifaceted outreach to the broken. Comiskey's ministry grows out of his commitment to overcome homosexuality and his experience as the husband of Annette and as the father of four grown children and eight grandchildren. He is author of *Pursuing Sexual Wholeness, Strength in Weakness, Naked Surrender,* and the Living Waters healing program. Andrew seeks to equip the global Church to be whole and holy, a Bride ready to receive Jesus. Andrew and Annette live in Kansas City, Missouri, where Andrew attends and serves in a local parish.

Sophia Institute

Sophia Institute is a nonprofit institution that seeks to nurture the spiritual, moral, and cultural life of souls and to spread the gospel of Christ in conformity with the authentic teachings of the Roman Catholic Church.

Sophia Institute Press fulfills this mission by offering translations, reprints, and new publications that afford readers a rich source of the enduring wisdom of mankind.

Sophia Institute also operates the popular online resource CatholicExchange.com. *Catholic Exchange* provides world news from a Catholic perspective as well as daily devotionals and articles that will help readers to grow in holiness and live a life consistent with the teachings of the Church.

In 2013, Sophia Institute launched Sophia Institute for Teachers to renew and rebuild Catholic culture through service to Catholic education. With the goal of nurturing the spiritual, moral, and cultural life of souls, and an abiding respect for the role and work of teachers, we strive to provide materials and programs that are at once enlightening to the mind and ennobling to the heart; faithful and complete, as well as useful and practical.

Sophia Institute gratefully recognizes the Solidarity Association for preserving and encouraging the growth of our apostolate over the course of many years. Without their generous and timely support, this book would not be in your hands.

www.SophiaInstitute.com
www.CatholicExchange.com
www.SophiaInstituteforTeachers.org

Sophia Institute Press is a registered trademark of Sophia Institute.
Sophia Institute is a tax-exempt institution as defined by the
Internal Revenue Code, Section 501(c)(3). Tax ID 22-2548708.